Beginning Teaching Workbook 3

Block Teaching Practice

Harry Tolley

Mary Biddulph

Tony Fisher

University of Nottingham

Chris Kington Publishing

CAMBRIDGE

© Harry Tolley
Mary Biddulph
Tony Fisher
1996

ISBN 1 899857 13 3

First published 1996 by
Chris Kington Publishing
27 Rathmore Road
Cambridge CB1 4AB

British Library cataloguing in publication data. A catalogue record for this book is available from the British Library.

Design by Thomas & Avery
Copy-editing by Carole Drummond, Milestone Editorial

Printed in the United Kingdom by York Publishing Services,
64 Hallfield Road, Layerthorpe, York YO3 7XQ

CONTENTS

FOREWORD

The responsibility for ITT and the professional development of new entrants to teaching lies increasingly with schools and colleges. Recent changes have created varied and flexible routes into teaching, through schemes such as the Licensed Teacher Scheme and School Centred Initial Teacher Training. Thus at this time when schools and colleges are having to cope with a whole host of other changes, they are also being asked to think afresh about how best they can manage and support the development of beginning teachers. In response they have become key stakeholders in new partnership arrangements with other schools and ITT institutions, and have created new management and support roles. The aim of *The Professional Development Management File* (of which this workbook is an integral part) is to provide guidance and resources for those involved in the school-based aspects of training and developing beginning teachers. These activities are worthwhile in their own right and active involvement in the development process is an important in-service experience for all those who participate in it, both as trainees and trainers. As such it contributes to the on-going development of staff and the creation of an environment in which working and professional learning are closely integrated.

Beginning Teaching Workbook 3 has been written to support those who are well established in their ITE programme and are now faced with a period of teaching practice in a school. As such it provides practical guidance on such crucial matters as developing a support network, finding out about the school as an organisation, conducting a teaching resources audit, devising schemes of work, preparing lessons, classroom management, developing professional competence, monitoring progress, finding out about the curriculum including the relevant stages of the National Curriculum. Underpinning the series is the view that beginning teachers should be encouraged to take increasing responsibility for the planning and management of their own learning.

The Beginning Teaching Workbooks have been written and designed to encourage their active use by individual beginning teachers. Materials such as checklists, proformas and competency profiles may be used to make OHP transparencies and/or supplementary copies for use in association with the workbooks.

INTRODUCTION

Aims

This workbook, *Beginning Teaching Workbook 3*, aims to support you in an extended period of teaching practice. We assume that before starting to use this book you will have:

- *made contact with your placement school and orientated yourself by finding out about it;*
- *established a working relationship (and ideally a learning partnership) with your mentor;*
- *undertaken some systematic, structured observation;*
- *planned, undertaken and evaluated some small group and whole class teaching;*
- *established a way of working within the 'plan/do/review' cyclical model of reflective practice;*
- *thought about your own professional learning as a beginning teacher;*
- *begun to read systematically about aspects of education;*
- *begun keeping some form of reflective journal.*

All of these aspects are covered in *Beginning Teaching Workbook 2*, to which we refer you for further detail.

Beginning Teaching Workbook 2: Beginning Initial Teacher Training

Workbook 3 now provides you with:

- *support for thinking about sequences of lessons, including the development of schemes of work;*
- *support for developing your thinking about methodology, resources and differentiation;*
- *suggestions for deepening your understanding of teaching and learning;*
- *suggestions for developing your thinking about some aspects of the broader curriculum;*
- *support for taking on wider aspects of the role of the teacher;*
- *some suggestions to help you to continue to maximise your professional learning and to manage the increased workload you will encounter.*

Achieving the aims

As indicated in the above section, we are assuming that you have certain things 'in place' in order to make an effective start on this next phase of your development towards **qualified teacher status** (QTS). Turn to **Figure 1** to see what we will be working through in this workbook.

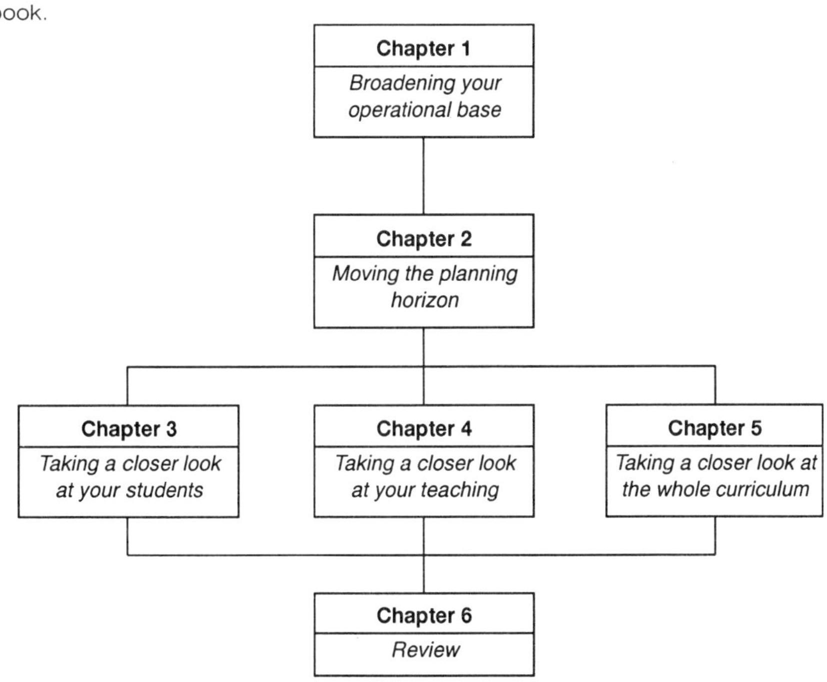

```
┌─────────────────────────┐
│       Chapter 1         │
├─────────────────────────┤
│    Broadening your      │
│    operational base     │
└─────────────────────────┘
             │
┌─────────────────────────┐
│       Chapter 2         │
├─────────────────────────┤
│    Moving the planning  │
│         horizon         │
└─────────────────────────┘
```

Chapter 3	Chapter 4	Chapter 5
Taking a closer look at your students	Taking a closer look at your teaching	Taking a closer look at the whole curriculum

```
┌─────────────────────────┐
│       Chapter 6         │
├─────────────────────────┤
│         Review          │
└─────────────────────────┘
```

Figure 1 Structure of *Beginning Teaching Workbook 3*

Beginning Teaching Workbook 2 concluded with some review activities leading into action planning to support this next phase of your development. If you have not done this personal review and action planning yet, do it **now**! What we are trying to achieve by the above review is a situation in which you can feel confident in terms of where your strengths and achievements lie, and where you have systematically identified aspects for development. In this way review and action planning will provide a platform from which to begin this next phase of your development. It should enable you to approach the increased level of responsibility and work load which lies ahead of you as an **opportunity** rather than a threat, and to **anticipate** some of the demands rather than react to them as a series of crises. 'Progress, therefore, is not an accident but a necessity ...' (Herbert Spencer).

All of this implies having a sense of your own development as something in which you not only have a **stake**, but a **controlling interest**. It is also a question of refining and rendering more subtle your understanding of those processes often glibly generalised as 'teaching' and 'learning'. This will involve bringing a deconstructing eye to the roles of 'teacher' and 'student/pupil', and to the institution of 'the school'. This, as noted in *Beginning Teaching Workbook 2*, will involve you in **reflection** and **critical thinking** about the situations in which you are simultaneously working and learning. If you are to achieve this, you need to be in a position where your *modus operandi* is one of active investigation rather than mere survival!

There is a balance to be found here. It is possible to investigate certain aspects of the teaching/learning complex in greater detail on a sort of 'Russian dolls' principle. This involves opening something up to find that inside it there is a more detailed aspect to investigate which, upon investigation, can be opened up to reveal a more detailed aspect .... There is nothing wrong with this – indeed, it is the very stuff of many an action research project, and yields fascinating insights and further questions. However, it is also important not to lose sight of 'the big picture' within which the teaching/learning complex is situated, comprising:

- *ideologies;*
- *political decisions;*
- *power distribution and relationships;*
- *social, technological and economic trends and developments.*

To have time to think about such things as a beginning teacher (and it is right that you should), implies that you will be 'on top of' the development of basic aspects of your work. *Beginning Teaching Workbook 2* endeavoured to provide you with some assistance in this direction and this workbook will continue in the same vein, helping you towards mastery of those aspects of a teacher's work which can be described as the craft of the classroom. However, as we have already indicated (*Beginning Teaching Workbook 2*), there is more to being a good teacher than merely being a good technician in a range of craft skills. Marland (1975, p 100) identifies that 'the craft won't work without a spirit compounded of the salesman, the music-hall performer, the parent, the clown, the intellectual, the lover and the organizer ...'. We might want to debate some of the items in the list (!), but the point is well made. Equally, 'the spirit won't win through on its own,' so technical mastery of craft aspects has a part to play (see the list of competencies on pages 46–50, for example).

The Teaching Competency Profile on pages 46–50 contains a list of competencies.

In *Beginning Teaching Workbook 2* we emphasised that teaching (and learning) can be seen as an interplay of cognitive, behavioural and affective aspects. MacIntyre in Bell and Day (1991) identifies honesty, courage and justice as key virtues characterising good practice in teaching, thus providing a moral or ethical dimension (and in so doing, linking the cognitive and affective 'domains'). In this book you will be asked to examine your own practice honestly and bravely, with a view to acting on the findings.

Action points

1. Look over your current action plan. Take steps to meet any short-term targets.
2. Review the situation *vis-à-vis* key dates (eg for handing in assignments).
3. Go through the check list in **Figure 2** and put right any deficiencies.

1. Have I checked with my mentor about my participation in any whole school programme for student teachers? ☐

2. Have I received my teaching timetable for this placement? ☐

3. Have I given copies of my timetable to anyone needing it, eg HE tutor? ☐

4. Have I observed/taught/discussed the class/es with which I am to work? ☐

5. Have I got name lists for all the classes/groups I am to teach? ☐

6. Have I got information (if appropriate) about individual abilities to enable me to consider the range of needs in my teaching groups? (see also 'Differentiation' on page 21). ☐

7. Have I got information about special needs support for individual pupils, including names of staff involved and nature and timing of support? ☐

8. Have I got the curricular aims and schemes of work for my class/es and do I know what I am responsible for teaching, when, how and at what level? (see also 'school procedures' on page 8). ☐

9. Am I fully conversant with the appropriate marking, assessment and recording procedures? (See also *Beginning Teaching Workbook 2*, Chapter 3). ☐

10. Am I familiar with expectations about work and conduct, and the use of rewards and sanctions? ☐

11. Do I know to whom to refer students/pupils, should the need arise? ☐

12. Do I know the emergency procedures in case of fire, injury and illness? (see also 'school procedures' on page 8). ☐

13. Do I know the buildings, their layout and points of access so that I can move easily from place to place as necessary? (see also 'Your familiarity with the school building and grounds' on page 7). ☐

14. Do I have a sketch plan of my teaching room/s, together with notes about possibilities/limitations regarding: seating arrangements; use of teaching aids; electrical supply points; display space; location of resources; blackout facilities? (see also page 6). ☐

15. Do I know the booking system for audio-visual aids and procedures re use/maintenance? ☐

16. Am I familiar with policy and procedures for the use of information technology (IT) and the location and availability of the school's hardware and software? ☐

17. Am I clear about my use of the school's reprographic facilities, including procedures and any restrictions? ☐

18. Have I met the school coordinator for student teacher placements? ☐

19. Am I clear about my participation in meetings (subject and other), parents' evenings and extra-curricular activities? (see also 'Your position in the communication/information networks of the school' on page 7). ☐

20. Am I clear about what is expected of me regarding attachment to a form/tutor group? (see also 'The pastoral aspect of your role' on page 4). ☐

Figure 2 Twenty questions: a check list for the start of a period of teaching practice

1

Broadening your operational base

Aims

Beginning Teaching Workbook 2 introduced you to a number of aspects of working in a school, on a deliberately small and manageable scale. You should now build on this by developing a much more extensive operational base. In the six sections of this chapter we will therefore:

- examine the pastoral aspect of your role;
- extend your support network;
- carry out a full audit of resources;
- develop your familiarity with the school buildings and grounds;
- consolidate your position in the communication/information networks of the school;
- develop your familiarity with school procedures.

The pastoral aspect of your role

*'I am a teacher more than a geographer, and a person more than a teacher' (Robin Richardson, in **Daring to be a Teacher**).*

There is a clear distinction here between the primary and secondary phases. Normally in the primary school the class teacher works with the same group of children all day and every day, from arrival to departure. In this situation the pastoral aspects of the teacher's work are closely bound up with all the others. We could say that the primary teacher is well placed to see 'the whole child in the whole curriculum'. Working with such a teacher, you will begin to work in a similar way. In such a holistic view of the teacher's work it may be difficult to isolate a distinct pastoral role.

*Perhaps inevitably, the structural arrangement described here has led to a dichotomised view of the academic and pastoral roles of the secondary teacher. This is particularly the case if you see your role as a **teacher of a subject** first and foremost. Then the pastoral aspect of the role can seem rather 'bolted on'.*
*If on the other hand you see yourself as a **teacher of young people** who happens sometimes to work through a subject medium to support their development, you will see the pastoral role as a perfectly natural part of your work.*
How do you see your 'core task' as a teacher?
How do you feel about the quotation from Robin Richardson?

The secondary school is very different. The whole curriculum is broken up into subjects, taught by different teachers. If you are working in a secondary school it is likely that you will be teaching no more than two, and often just one, of these subjects. Though you will still have the needs of the whole child at heart, you are not going to get to know each individual you teach as well or as rapidly as the typical primary teacher. In addition to your teaching timetable, you will probably also be allocated a **form** or **tutor group** with which to work. If you are not, ask to be. As such, you will be part of a **pastoral team** comprising a tutor team working with a Year Head or Head of House.

This will give you a different perspective on the role of the teacher because in this context you will not have a 'subject' to 'teach'. You will spend registration time with your form and perhaps you will have enough time to be involved in some structured activities designed to support their **personal and social development** (PSD) as individuals, in addition to necessary administration and messages. There may be timetabled tutor time for you to spend with your form, and a school programme of **personal and social education** (PSE) in which you will become involved (see also page 43).

Action point

Talk to your mentor about your responsibilities *vis-à-vis* the pastoral aspect of the role, and what support you will receive in discharging those responsibilities. In the secondary school, ask to be put in touch with the Head of Year/Head of House with whom you will be working.

Extending your support network

In *Beginning Teaching Workbook 2* we looked briefly at aspects of the working relationship between you and your mentor. We indicated that ideally this relationship would be seen by you both as a 'learning partnership', and clearly should be of great importance to you as a source of advice and support. On the other hand, you will not want to over-burden your mentor, and part of functioning autonomously in a school is about knowing who else can provide the support you will inevitably need (and part of belonging to a school community is also about giving support and help to others). The following list, which though lengthy is not exhaustive, gives you some pointers:

Other teachers. This will vary according to the school in which you are teaching. In the primary school your mentor is probably the class teacher with whom you are working for most of the time. Your mentor and the other teachers in the school may have one or more National Curriculum subjects to coordinate. Find out who is responsible for which subject/s so that you can approach them directly when you need to. If it is a fairly small school, staffroom conversation may be a whole staff affair. Listen and join in. In a larger secondary school you will probably be placed in a subject department. Here you will probably work not only with your designated mentor but also with his or her department colleagues. In this case your mentor will coordinate the way his or her subject colleagues work with you, including the collation of views and information for the writing of profiles and reports. Effectively the mentoring role will be shared within the department. You will meet other teachers through the pastoral/tutor aspect of your role and also if you get involved in activities outside this and your subject responsibilities. This will enable you to have a broader range of staffroom contacts. In a large staffroom, whole-staff conversation is impractical, so having more contacts gives you access to more groups.

The school coordinator/professional tutor. If you are in a school which has several 'student teachers', your placement and the work of mentors may be coordinated by a designated member of staff. In some schools this will be a Deputy Head Teacher. This is to some degree an administrative role, but it may also involve him or her working directly with you as an individual or, more usually, as a group. Such a member of staff may also have an overall responsibility for the induction of **newly qualified teachers** (NQTs). He or she is a good person with whom to discuss broader educational matters, but may be very busy!

Support teachers. You are most likely to encounter these teachers if they are working with children you teach. Some schools have 'Section 11 teachers' who are designated to work with children for whom English is not their first language. Other kinds of support teachers are allocated to work with certain children such as those designated as having 'special needs'. These children require additional support, either in class or on a withdrawal basis.

Union representative. You may have taken out student membership of one or more of the teachers' unions and professional associations (indeed, we recommend that you do so). Find out which members of the teaching staff are the representatives/contact points. This is a voluntary role, sometimes elected by the union members in the school. Such representatives are useful sources of information on professional matters, and can put you in contact with local officers of the organisation.

School librarian. If you are in a school which has a librarian, this can be to your advantage. He or she can provide help with materials and resources for teaching and learning, project collections and reading lists. You can also seek help with the development of information retrieval and study skills. He or she may also be able to help with your own reading if there is a staff collection or 'professional matters' shelf, and act as a link with local library services.

School nurse. If you are in a school with a school nurse (normally the larger schools) you can seek support with aspects of personal and health education, including sex education. In addition the school nurse carries out health inspections and coordinates the work of visiting health teams, eg for vaccinations. In a smaller school a nurse may visit on a rota basis.

Technical staff. These are not normally found in the primary sector. They include laboratory technicians and workshop technicians. Their work is normally restricted to support in designated subject areas, eg science and technology. If you are lucky there may be someone designated to help staff as an audio-visual technician, but do not bank on it!

Administrative, secretarial and reprographic staff. It is important to get to know these staff. Again, just how many there are and what they do will vary from school to school. A small primary school may run to some part-time secretarial support only, whereas a large comprehensive school may have a bursar/administrator, several secretaries, a receptionist/ switchboard operator and a reprographics department!

The school caretaker. This can be a very useful member of staff to know, particularly in a

What's in a name? (1)
Some teachers have an officially designated role of **mentor**. *The school has selected them to work with you. On the other hand, it is possible to conceive of the whole thing much more flexibly, where several staff share the mentoring role. One may coordinate the support and assessment, but they are* **all** *to a degree your mentors and share the mentoring functions of: teaching; sponsoring; encouraging; counselling; befriending. What matters is that these functions of mentoring are fulfilled, and in some cases this will be by people who are not officially your mentor at all. Ultimately you will seek advice etc from someone with whom you feel comfortable, regardless of whether they are your designated mentor or not.*

What's in a name? (2)
Your turn! Elsewhere in these books we have referred to you as a 'beginner teacher' or 'beginning teacher'. In some schools you'll be a 'teaching student', often just plain 'student' (and, less frequently, a 'student teacher'). In some places you will be referred to as an 'intern', in others as a 'novice teacher'. What would you call yourself? Does it matter?

smaller school. In the larger secondary school with its more clearly demarcated roles and responsibilities you are less likely to have direct contact with the caretaker, but if you are in school early or after the school day has finished you may meet as they do their rounds, so introduce yourself (and avoid getting locked in!).

The Head Teacher. Through pressure of work and the complexity of this role he or she is not usually in a position to give you much direct support or assistance, though in a small primary school you are likely to have more day to day contact with her or him than in a large secondary school. If you have not yet met the Head and no formal meeting is scheduled, go and introduce yourself. (Check with the school office staff about protocol – some Heads operate an 'open door' policy where you can simply drop in unannounced, whereas others have a diary of appointments. Either way, you are working in his or her school, so it is right that you at least meet!)

Action points

1.　Having read the above, draw up a list of the appropriate staff you need to meet. Find out their names and set a deadline for meeting them all.
2.　In addition to supporting you, some of the staff listed here may well welcome some support and assistance from you. Whilst not suggesting that you start to do other people's jobs for them, giving a small amount of assistance in a way which is useful to them may well also give you useful insights into how your school functions. Explore the possibilities.

The resources audit

Beginning Teaching Workbook 2 had quite a lot to say about resources of one sort and another. This was largely set in the context of preparing the individual lesson. Your circumstances are now different. In order to be able to function autonomously during a sustained teaching practice you need to have a comprehensive view of what is available by way of resources, where they are stored and how to get hold of the ones you want to use. That is why we suggest that you now carry out a full resources 'audit'.

Activity

Spend some time looking systematically through the range of resources available for you to use in your teaching. You will find it useful to note:

- *where the item/s in question are stored;*
- *what the booking system and/or conditions of use (including safety) are for any technical equipment, sets of books, etc;*
- *other useful information, eg from whom to seek technical advice or support, 'watch points', critical notes, etc.*

Construct your own resources audit framework bearing in mind the points above. You will need to include some of the suggested resources listed below. (Your precise list will reflect your circumstances: primary/secondary; subject, etc.)

- *books, including textbooks, class readers, atlases, dictionaries, etc;*
- *worksheets/work cards;*
- *other materials (eg maps, sets of photographs, diagrams, wall charts);*
- *subject-specific equipment (eg musical instruments, scientific apparatus, PE equipment, tools, a weather station);*
- *audio-visual equipment including a video playback, an overhead projector (OHP), a slide projector, tape recorders, a video camera;*
- *information technology (IT) including computers, a CD-ROM player, and software, (including simulations, CD-ROMs, etc);*
- *artefacts;*

- simulation activities;
- chalk/drywipe board;
- general classroom resources (eg plain, lined and squared paper, hole punch, stapler and staples, scissors, glue, crayons, spare pens, pencils and paints);
- display materials (backing paper, trigger tacker and staples, display pins);
- replacement exercise books/files, jotters (and procedures for issue).

Action point

File the results of your resources audit with your lesson planning materials.

Your familiarity with the school buildings and grounds

You have a teaching commitment. In the primary school this means you will be allocated to a classroom. In the secondary school it is likely that you will teach in more than one room. You should have a plan of the school. Investigate other spaces which you could use for teaching and learning, in addition to your timetabled teaching space. For each space, find out and note how you can get access to that space (eg booking arrangements), should you wish to use it. Here are some you might consider (do not assume that all schools have all of these!):

- the hall;
- the library/resources centre;
- a computer room;
- a drama space/studio/theatre;
- a lecture theatre/audio-visual room;
- social spaces/year or house bases;
- the gymnasium/sports hall;
- a design area/art room;
- other classrooms (you may be able to negotiate access for specific reasons, eg your room does not have black-out facilities and you want to swap to one which does for a lesson with slides);
- the school grounds (eg hard areas, pitches, wildlife areas, etc);
- any other useful areas, inside or out, which may be particular to your school.

Action point

You have just conducted what might be thought of as a 'premises audit'. File your findings with the results of your resources audit. And remember: whichever space you use, leave it as you found it.

Your position in the communication/information networks of the school

If you are to function autonomously in your school it is vital that you are embraced in the school's communications network. It is to no one's advantage if all communications are channelled through your mentor (some will inevitably be, however). Again, this is less likely to be complicated in the smaller school, but nevertheless there are things you will not want to leave to chance. The larger the school, the more complex the network is likely to be, and your place in it should be clear to all concerned, including yourself. Some aspects may be covered in the staff handbook (we suggested in Chapter 2 'First encounters' of *Beginning Teaching Workbook 2* that you get a copy of this). You may have done some of the following already, so use the action points below as a check list.

Action points

1. Ensure that the secretarial staff know who you are and who your mentor is, in case they have to take an in-coming message for you (eg from your HE tutor).

Schools as organisations

There are sometimes 'territories' present in a school. These may or may not be visible, but it is advisable to be sensitive to their existence. A member of staff who has a particular responsibility for looking after an area may give the impression that it actually belongs to him or her. It does not of course, but it is a good idea to bear his or her feelings in mind when seeking access to that space. Some staffrooms too have territories within them. This may not be desirable, but in some schools it is a fact of life. Again it is advisable to be aware of the possibility and to check it out. Many classrooms in a secondary school are used as form rooms for registration etc, in addition to their subject use. This can lead to issues around the use of notice boards. Some rooms may also be used as social areas at break times which may at times be incompatible with other uses.

2. Ensure that your mentor and the school office have your home telephone number and that you have the school's number at home (eg to let them know if you are ill) and with you when you are in transit (eg to warn them if you are delayed in your journey).

3. Many schools now have staff briefings (eg before school begins in the morning). Find out if yours does and if so, when they are so you can be sure to attend.

4. Get a calendar of meetings and discuss attendance at meetings with the relevant staff. In principle we feel it is best for you to attend a full range of meetings in order to gain as much insight into the school, its procedures and concerns as possible. The assumption is that you will attend meetings unless asked specifically not to, rather than wait to be individually invited – but be sure to clarify this with relevant staff first.

5. Ensure that you visit the staffroom every day. This is particularly important if you are working in a large school and the staffroom is in a different part of the school from your teaching 'patch'.

6. Find out if there is a 'pigeon hole' system for mail and communications to and between staff. If there is, ask if you can have a pigeon hole too, and clear it regularly (at least once per day).

7. Find out about the notice board system. Who puts notices up? Who takes them down and after how long? Is there a 'white board' or other system for current/urgent items? Check it at least once per day. Where are the union/professional association noticeboards?

8. You will want to contact those whom you teach from time to time outside lessons. Find out how this is done in your school (eg via notes in the register, daily briefings etc).

9. Find out about the protocol and procedures for communicating with parents, either over individual matters or as a group (eg regarding a visit out of school). Note that we do not envisage that you will independently make contact with parents at this stage. Always refer to your mentor/form tutor for advice.

Your familiarity with school procedures

All schools have explicit procedures by which the organisation endeavours to ensure its smooth and safe running. It is important that you should be aware of these procedures and follow them as appropriate. Many of these procedures will be found in the staff handbook.

Action points

1. Ensure that you know what to do in the following circumstances:

- *a child in your class feels ill;*
- *a child draws your attention to a broken window;*
- *there is an accident at break time and someone is lying on the ground;*
- *the fire alarm sounds;*
- *someone in a class you are teaching arrives late;*
- *there is a fight in the corridor;*
- *an incident involving racist name-calling is reported to you;*
- *someone you are teaching says they have to leave now for a dentist's appointment;*
- *someone hands you a piece of lost property;*
- *you want to arrange a visit out of school;*
- *someone whom you are teaching is upset and cannot be consoled;*
- *an unidentified visitor asks to be directed to his or her son or daughter;*
- *you find an area of floor which has become a safety hazard;*
- *you want a television broadcast to be recorded;*
- *you want a class set of copies of a worksheet you have devised;*

After working through this activity it is worth considering whether there are any general strategies which you can apply in the face of unexpected problems and issues.

- *a member of your class who normally brings sandwiches has forgotten their lunch.*

There are a hundred and one other situations we could put on this list, and inevitably something will catch you unprepared, but try to be prepared for as many foreseeable eventualities as possible.

2. One particularly important procedure of which to be aware is related to **child abuse**. Every school is required by law to have a designated member of staff who is the link person in actual or suspected cases of child abuse. He or she will have received training in his or her responsibilities. Here is a summary of **your** responsibilities:

   - *you should ensure that you know who the designated person is;*
   - *if you have any suspicions or concerns, you have a legal obligation to inform the designated member of staff;*

If a child says that they want to tell you something private (and there are many ways of them letting you know this), you should tell them that, depending on what it is, you may have to tell someone else. Do not worry if at this point the child decides not to pursue the matter. That is their right, as any such information 'belongs to them'. However, if the child then discloses to you, you should:

- *believe them;*
- *let them tell you in their way;*
- *let them stop if they cannot continue;*
- *stop them when you are clear about what they are telling you;*
- *tell them that it is not their fault;*
- *tell them that they have done the right thing in letting you know;*
- *tell them that you will have to tell someone else (the designated person);*
- *make detailed notes immediately after the disclosure and sign and date them;*
- *inform the designated person as soon as possible (note that it is an offence not to pass on the information, even if the discloser says he or she does not want you to!)*

In addition, you should:

- *resist any impulse to question, prompt or 'lead' them to help them disclose;*
- *resist any temptation to reassure them that everything will be all right;*
- *resist any temptation to offer a judgement (eg 'he or she should not have done that');*
- *retain confidentiality, apart from informing the designated person;*
- *seek support personally if you feel affected by what has happened.*

An awareness of procedures around child abuse and child protection is now very much part of a teacher's job. Support for teachers is available through in-service training.
Children can seek support through Childline. The National Society for the Prevention of Cruelty to Children and specially trained police officers take a key role in cases to be investigated.

Summary

In this chapter we have endeavoured to support you in broadening your operational base with regard to the pastoral role, other staff, resources, spaces, communication and procedures. You may by now be feeling a bit shell-shocked by the complexity of the role you have taken on. Everyone in teaching, including the authors, was once in the same position! Please be reassured that you will learn all these things (and more!) and you will cope.

Sometimes you will have to ask for advice, and there is nothing wrong with that. No one expects you to know everything. There is a balance to be struck between being self-reliant and making realistic use of others' knowledge and expertise. What you should try to avoid is the position in which you are over-dependent. This will inhibit your learning and be burdensome for those with whom you work. But recognise that teaching today is complex, and complex issues are best tackled by teams bringing their various individual strengths to bear cooperatively on the shared enterprise. A school is, after all, a community, and no one can expect more of you than that you function as a responsible, caring member of that community.

2
Moving the planning horizon

Aims

In this section we aim to get you thinking about the relationship between lessons in terms of progression and continuity. This will enable you to think of a 'planning horizon' beyond the requirements for the individual lesson and to begin to develop a sense of where the lessons are going. This will enable us to consider 'schemes of work' as key elements of curriculum planning, whatever the context in terms of key stage and subject.

Progression

In *Beginning Teaching Workbook 2* we introduced you to some detailed considerations regarding lesson planning but of course lessons are not normally free standing, unconnected events. Normally they form part of a sequence in which they will be connected to others. In this way it is important to consider **progression** and **continuity** in a sequence of lessons.

Progression refers to the **development** of the sequence. It may be present in one or more of the following aspects:

● *The development of a sequence may reflect the stages of the learning cycle which we referred to in* Beginning Teaching Workbook 2 *(see* Figure 2.1*);*
● *Progression may correspond to an increase in the level of complexity of information to be handled or concepts to be understood;*
● *It may correspond to the level of difficulty of skills to be developed or of problems to be solved;*
● *It may be present in the amount and nature of teacher support offered/withheld;*
● *Another dimension of progression may be in the cognitive level (level of thinking) at which the learner is required to operate. One way of looking at this is the application of a framework such as that provided by Bloom's Taxonomy of educational objectives (see* Figure 2.2*). In this approach cognitive operations are ordered from the simplest ('knowledge') to the most complex ('evaluation').*

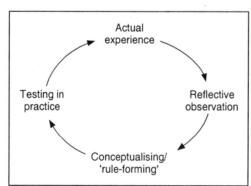
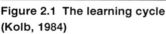
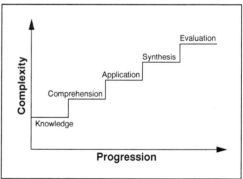

Figure 2.1 The learning cycle (Kolb, 1984)

Figure 2.2 Progression of educational objectives (Bloom, 1956)

Clearly progression is a complex aspect of planning for learning. It would be a mistake to think of it as purely linear. Observing children learning will tell you that! Also, a purely linear view would be incompatible with the idea of the learning cycle. Reinforcement and practice are important consolidating elements in learning. Some teachers therefore think of learning as a succession of cycles and extend the idea to speak of a 'spiral curriculum' in which ideas and topics are reencountered at increasing levels of sophistication (eg some topics from *Beginning Teaching Workbook 2* reappear here and later in the series).

Progression also takes place over differing time frames in the form of gradual transitions. No one would disagree that as an adult your knowledge base, cognitive skills and conceptual frameworks are vastly more sophisticated than they were when you were, say, five years old. But just exactly what was the nature of the journey? Can you chart your trajectory as a learner, and, more importantly, explain **how** you progressed? It is not so easy, even as an educated adult, to be able to engage in 'metacognition' (thinking about thinking). Yet it is this slippery notion of progression in learning that we are trying to get a grip on as teachers, in order to be able to support those whom we teach appropriately to their needs.

The writers of the National Curriculum have attempted to describe progression in each of the **attainment targets** by providing **level descriptions**. A level description is a paragraph of text which summarises performance at that level in terms of knowledge, understanding and skills (see also *Beginning Teaching Workbook 2*). The idea here is that it should be possible to apply these descriptions to children's performance in those subjects on a 'best fit' basis rather than by an exact match. So, though this is in essence a linear, stepwise view of progression, there is an inbuilt admission that progression is not as neat as eight levels per attainment target might suggest, hence the idea of 'best fit'.

Activity

A practical way of investigating progression is to use the following reading activity, which you may also like to use in your own lesson planning if appropriate (**Sequencing**, as it is called, has many applications when you want students to read text closely to identify an underlying thread, eg a chronological sequence or a chain of cause and effect.) In the case of this activity it is best if someone else does the preparation for you to avoid you inadvertently reading the text!

● *Choose a National Curriculum subject which is familiar to you;*
● *Select an attainment target (some have only one) and photocopy the level descriptions;*
● *Cut them into nine separate strips, remove the headings and shuffle them;*
● *Read them and reassemble the sequence from Level 1 to 'exceptional performance';*
● *Check your sequence against the original;*
● *Reflect on the nature of progression in your chosen subject. Is it clear? Can you foresee any potential benefits or problems in applying this version of progression in your teaching situation?*

Continuity

Continuity means what it says. It is the necessary link between aspects of the learning which is taking place. Continuity can take any of the following forms (normally several in combination):

● *theme (topic), eg the primary school teacher may establish continuity of theme through a term's work by linking all activities to a topic title or focus;*
● *subject material, eg a sequence of lessons in, say, science, investigating enzymes;*
● *narrative (the continuity of a story-line or plot);*
● *chronological sequence (not the exclusive property of history!);*
● *methodology, ie doing things the same way over a period of time to reinforce a sense of continuity. (If combined with the idea of building explicitly this achieves progression as well, eg skill development in music or sport);*
● *experience, ie is the learner's sense of continuity reinforced through his or her experiences?*
● *relationships, eg working with the same group;*
● *recording, ie the developing record of a student's work and progress kept by the teacher, and by the student via a record of achievement (ROA).*

Of course neither progression nor continuity should be looked on as something which must, at all times and in every way, be adhered to. But both should obviously underlie our planning, and are very important criteria in curriculum evaluation. When we do depart from them it must be for a demonstrably good reason.

Activity

In conjunction with your mentor, identify a topic or theme which you are going to teach. Plan an outline sequence of lessons on the topic, paying particular attention to progression and continuity. The approximate length of the sequence will depend on individual circumstances and should be negotiated with your mentor. Do not produce detailed lesson plans at this stage. You should indicate the following:

- *the target age of the group/class;*
- *the main theme (chosen from appropriate National Curriculum programme/s of study);*
- *the overall aim/s and key learning objectives of the sequence, but not the specific lesson objectives;*
- *the anticipated range of attainment (see level descriptions);*
- *the number of lessons/time-scale;*
- *the main focus of each lesson;*
- *the key resources and equipment.*

Note: your sequence of lessons need not (indeed probably should not) cover all aspects of the relevant descriptions.

Discuss your outline sequence of lessons with your mentor. Remember that it is only an outline at this stage. There are other important considerations to be borne in mind when planning the detail, as we shall see.

Schemes of work

The outline sequence of lessons you planned in the previous activity is close to being a 'scheme of work'. Such schemes of work have two purposes:

- *they provide an explicit, clear and formal framework for the more detailed planning of individual lessons;*
- *they provide information to teachers, the school's senior managers and governors, parents and inspectors about the nature of the curriculum.*

In the case of planning for subjects of the National Curriculum, schemes of work provide a necessary link between the **programme of study** (PoS) and the individual lesson. In the case of examination syllabuses the function of the scheme of work is essentially similar.

What the programme of study and the examination syllabus have in common is that they specify **what** is to be studied during a key stage or during an examination course, but they go no further in terms of:

- *how to divide the 'work' into sections of clear focus and coherence (though there are exceptions to this, eg the history study units of the programme of study for history);*
- *the links which may be made or explored with work in other subject areas;*
- *how to combine elements of the work with one another to enhance the learning opportunities;*
- *how much time to give to 'topics' and to individual elements;*
- *the sequence of topics;*
- *the sequence of lessons within a given topic;*
- *the methodologies to be used;*
- *the sorts of learning activities which may be planned;*
- *the resources to be used;*
- *how the work is to be made accessible to students with a range of abilities, and how the work is to be made challenging across the ability range;*
- *the on-going provision for informal assessment and feedback to students, and other evaluative procedures.*

In short, they do not outline **how** the subject is to be taught. This remains a matter for teachers, based on their local circumstances, and their views about their subject.

There is quite a lot of flexibility in this situation, with external accountability being exercised through end of key stage assessment (GCSE examinations at Key Stage 4) and through the OFSTED inspection framework. Parents may also ask to see schemes of work. Internal accountability is a matter for school and departmental procedures. There is no set 'template' to which schemes of work must conform but, by general agreement, they usually cover all or most of the aspects mentioned above. How they are set out varies from school to school, and sometimes within a school as well.

Activity (i)

1. Ask your mentor if you can see some schemes of work if you have not yet done so.
2. Look at the sections into which they are divided, and the nature of the information they contain.
3. Discuss the nature of these particular schemes of work with your mentor. What is the rationale behind the way they are organised and the information they contain?
4. Look again at your outline sequence of lessons. In the light of what you now know, what do you need to add to make your outline into a 'scheme of work'? Make the necessary additions and changes.

Clearly you will need to construct separate schemes of work for separate aspects of the teaching which is required of you. You may be in a position where the mentor hands you a scheme of work which you are then expected to teach. This may seem supportive, but it means that you are not on the inside of the planning decisions which lie behind the scheme. In such circumstances we suggest that you discuss with your mentor whether it would be possible for you to work to the same set of aims and key learning objectives but to come up with your own scheme of work (even if, in the end, it is not much different from the school's).

This may seem a bit like 'reinventing the wheel', but we feel strongly that you need this sort of experience in the supported context of a teaching practice if you are later to be able to take up the responsibility independently. So, if your mentor agrees, set the school's scheme aside and try not to let your thinking be influenced by what you have seen of it. Start from scratch; there is time to compare your thoughts with the school's **after** you have done the thinking and planning, and who knows, you may surprise yourself by improving on what the school does. Many schools value having students on teaching practice for the very reason that it can bring fresh perspectives to an established situation, so do not underestimate your potential for making a contribution. On the other hand, do not arrogantly assume that you know best!

Activity (ii)

The next step is of course to turn your scheme of work into fully planned lessons with clearly identified objectives. It may be tempting to plan all the lessons for a whole scheme ahead of time, but whilst this might be laudable from the point of view of personal organisation, it would deprive you of a certain amount of flexibility to modify your plans in the light of experience. As a compromise we therefore suggest the following:

●   *Make arrangements to have access to any resources required for your scheme of work. This will include booking any necessary audio-visual equipment, special rooms, etc, as appropriate;*
●   *Plan the first few lessons in detail. Use the lesson planning guidelines and framework from* **Beginning Teaching Workbook 2** *to support you in this;*
●   *Design and produce sufficient copies of any 'home-made' resources required for the lessons you have planned in detail;*
●   *Begin the drafting of other resources you anticipate using in later lessons;*
●   *Ensure that you have all the information you need about the classes to whom you will be teaching the lessons, eg lists of names;*
●   *Ensure that you have access to all necessary equipment, eg scissors, backing paper, other materials, etc;*

- Teach the first two or three lessons, reviewing and evaluating each lesson against its specific objectives;
- Review progress against the scheme of work, modifying later sections of the scheme as appropriate in the light of your experience in teaching the lessons;
- Continue with cycles of plan/do/review at the lesson and scheme of work level (see **Figure 2.3**) until you have completed the scheme;
- Review the scheme in its entirety and make any necessary amendments before filling it with other schemes and lesson plans for future use.

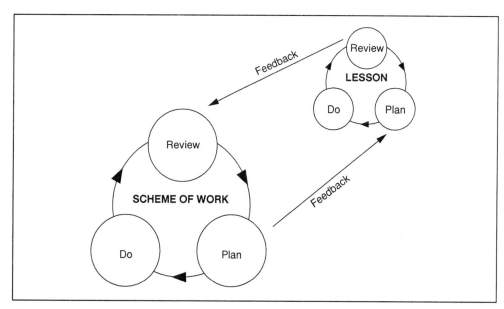

Figure 2.3 The relationship between plan/do/review cycles for individual lessons and the scheme of work to which they relate

Monitoring your teaching

Collecting evidence about your teaching (1)

Lesson plans are evidence of your intentions for a lesson. The matrix of approaches complements your growing collection of plans.

'Variety's the very spice of life, that gives it all its flavour' observed William Cowper, and this is certainly true of teaching. If your schemes of work, ideas about progression and continuity, lesson objectives and resources are the basic ingredients, then it is the methodological choices which you make which are your room for manoeuvre and therefore your source of variety, the spice to give your teaching flavour.

On page 15 is a matrix of teaching techniques and approaches (**Figure 2.4**). Its purpose is to enable you to monitor this aspect of your teaching. We suggest that you make a copy for each class you teach. Each time you take a lesson or teach a class, fill in the date in the next empty column and indicate which of the approaches you used. Regular review of the sheets will enable you to monitor your own use of these approaches.

Note that we are not suggesting that you should aim to use all of the approaches equally. That could result in some very contrived situations indeed. Inevitably there are some which you will use more than others, and there is nothing wrong with that. However, it is useful to be able to monitor whether or not you are over using a narrow range of strategies and to have a list of some possible alternatives.

Reviewing your teaching

It is important for you to review your teaching regularly, using information from a range of sources. The teaching matrix (**Figure 2.4**) we described above is one such source. Another source is the work you get from your students, including the motivation and enthusiasm they display. One very important source of information is from an observer in the classroom. Observation may or may not be the main reason why a person is there, but you can elicit very useful feedback from anyone who shares a classroom with you, be they your mentor,

Teaching approaches monitoring matrix†

Name of group .... Subject/topic..

National Curriculum year group .... Notes..

NB: Tick/code as many boxes per lesson as appropriate ....

Approach used	Date of lesson																	
Main focus on knowledge/understanding																		
Main focus on skill development																		
Main focus on attitudes/values																		
Discussion (p/g)*																		
Question/answer																		
Instruction/explanation																		
Creative writing																		
Comprehension/other written work																		
Number skills																		
Drama/role play																		
Simulation																		
Project work (i/p/g)*																		
Practical work (i/p/g)*																		
Work for display or presentation																		
Graphical work (dr/pt/im/de/di/m)*																		
Chalk/dry-wipe board																		
OHP																		
Text/workbooks																		
Information/worksheets																		
Video playback																		
Audio playback																		
Video camera																		
Tape recorder																		
Slides																		
Information technology																		
Library																		
Work outside the classroom																		
Team teaching (ct/st/os)*																		
Work marked																		
Lesson related to NC PoS																		

† Note: Does not include subject specific approaches

* Codes to be used: i: individual; p: pairs; g: group
> dr: drawing; pt: painting; im: imaginative; de: decorative; di: diagram; m: map
> ct: class teacher; st: support teacher; os: other student teacher

Figure 2.4 Matrix for monitoring teaching approaches and techniques

another class teacher, a support teacher, your tutor, or a fellow student teacher.

Of course, you are more likely to get useful feedback from them if you negotiate a clear brief, ie the aspect/s on which to concentrate and about which you want them to give you feedback. Do not ask them to make a judgement ('was it good?') but instead ask for factual information. This is potentially very useful, because when you are in the thick of some interactive teaching it is to all intents impossible to stand apart from yourself and analyse what you are doing.

When evaluating a lesson it is important to weigh the evidence and information rather than leap to a snap judgement. Try to resist the temptation. The reflective process needs time and fuel in the form of **information**, not merely a subjective impression. Entire lessons are very rarely simply good or bad so do not try to judge them in this way. Rather, let your evaluation be guided by your planning, in other words by the extent to which your objectives for the lesson were met. Though there is a place for 'subjective, impressionistic judgements', 'objective, criterion-based judgements' are likely to be more useful here. For more guidance on the evaluation of an individual lesson we refer you to *Beginning Teaching Workbook 2*.

Part of the process of conducting an on-going review of your teaching is to make sure that you use your evaluations as an input into your planning. It is also important to ensure that you gain an overview of your evaluations, and develop a realistic view of your own development of competencies which you can then check out in discussion with your mentor and tutor.

We are assuming here that you will be having regular review meetings with your mentor – the frequency will reflect individual circumstances – at which you discuss your progress. We suggest that if possible these meetings are scheduled in advance, and that their purpose is to review progress. This can only occur if you have a view about your own progress and areas of strength and relative weakness which can then provide a basis for target setting and action planning.

Action points

1.   Review the teaching you have done to date.
2.   If you have not yet had a review meeting with your mentor, try to arrange one now.

Collecting evidence about your teaching (2)
A formally set up and conducted observation should result in **written feedback** *on an observation schedule. The form of this varies greatly, from the blank sheet at one end of the scale to the tick-box schedule at the other. In our work we have found a compromise useful, and have included a copy of such an observation schedule on pages 51–54 (The Lesson Observation Schedule). You should always have a copy of such observation notes and keep it carefully with the appropriate lesson plan as another source of evidence.*

Whether or not you are observed in a lesson, you will also conduct your own **evaluations.** *These may be included on your lesson plans, or may be separate documents. Either way, they are further evidence about your teaching and should be systematically conducted and filed with the lesson plan.*

3
Taking a closer look at learning

Aims

It is a fact of life in teaching that though our students learn as individuals, we tend to encounter them as groups. Inevitably this leads to a tension between our need to plan for teaching them as groups (eg as set out by the scheme of work you planned in Chapter 2) and their need as learners to be treated as individuals.

In this chapter we are going to take a much closer look at learning and the way in which individuals differ from one another. This will involve examining your own preferred learning style. From that basis we aim to get you to think about the whole area of individual difference and individual learning needs, and conclude by getting you to think systematically about 'differentiation' as an essential characteristic of good teaching and learning.

Learning style

One way in which individual difference can be manifested is through preferred learning style. In *Beginning Teaching Workbook 2* we drew briefly on the work of Kolb in bringing the learning cycle to your attention. Kolb uses the four elements of the cycle (see also **Figure 2.1** of this workbook) to identify four basic learning modes:

- *concrete experience (actual experience);*
- *reflective observation;*
- *conceptualisation (conceptualising/'rule-forming');*
- *active experimentation (testing in practice).*

Kolb suggests that these learning modes are present in all of us, all four being necessary aspects of the learning cycle. However, the balance will vary from person to person, some of us having quite clear leanings or preferences towards one or more modes. There is nothing 'right' or 'wrong' about this as each has strengths and weaknesses. The ideal position is to be able to use each and any mode as appropriate in a particular set of circumstances, whether or not we display a preference, and whatever our preference may be. Your particular balance of modes is your personal learning style.

There are two reasons why this is important:

- *your preferred learning style can influence the ways in which you attempt to assist others;*
- *an individual's learning style affects his or her response to different sorts of learning activities and also the kind of help needed from you.*

Activity

Complete the following self-analysis questionnaire (**Figure 3.1**) which is designed to help you find your preferred learning style/s. It is based on an approach developed by The Careers and Occupational Information Centre (COIC) and which incorporates Kolb's ideas. The questionnaire works by the way your answers indicate a profile of your personality. From this profile aspects of your preferred learning style/s can be inferred. There are no right or wrong answers, but the accuracy of the results depends on how accurately you can answer, and this means making a truly honest response based on how you see yourself.

For each statement you should:

- *read and consider the statement as it applies to you;*
- *put a tick next to the statement if you agree more than you disagree with it;*
- *put a cross by it if you disagree more than you agree with it.*

Note that you must not miss out any statements because this will affect the result.

1. I like to be absolutely correct about things.
2. I quite like taking risks.
3. I prefer to solve problems using a step-by-step approach rather than guessing.
4. I prefer simple, straightforward things rather than something complicated.
5. I often do things 'just because I feel like it' rather than thinking about it first.
6. I don't often take things for granted. I like to check things out for myself.
7. What matters most about what you learn is whether it works in practice.
8. I actively seek out new things to do.
9. When I hear about a new idea I immediately start working out how I can try it out.
10. I am quite keen on sticking to fixed routines, keeping to timetables etc.
11. I take great care in working things out. I don't like jumping to conclusions.
12. I like to make decisions very carefully and preferably after weighing up all the other possibilities first.
13. I don't like 'loose-ends': I prefer to see things fit into some sort of pattern.
14. In discussions I like to get straight to the point.
15. I like the challenge of trying something new and different.
16. I prefer to think things through before coming to a conclusion.
17. I find it difficult to come up with wild ideas off the top of my head.
18. I prefer to have as many bits of information about a subject as possible: the more I have to sift through the better.
19. I prefer to jump in and do things as they come along rather than plan things out in advance.
20. I tend to judge other people's ideas on how they work in practice.
21. I don't think you can make a decision just because something 'feels' right: you have to think about all the facts.
22. I am rather fussy about how I do things – a bit of a perfectionist.
23. In discussion I usually pitch in with lots of wild ideas.
24. In discussions I only put forward ideas that I know will work.
25. I prefer to look at a problem from as many different angles as I can before starting on it.
26. Usually I talk more than I listen.
27. Quite often I can work out more practical ways of doing things.
28. I believe that careful, logical thinking is the key to getting things done.
29. If I have to write a formal letter I prefer to try out several rough workings before writing out the final version.
30. I like to consider all the alternatives before making up my mind.
31. I don't like wild ideas. They are not very practical.
32. It's best to look before you leap.
33. I usually do more listening than talking.
34. It doesn't matter how you do something, as long as it works.
35. I can't be bothered with rules and plans: they take all the 'fun' out of things.
36. I'm usually the 'life and soul of the party'.
37. I do whatever I need to do to get the job done.
38. I like to find out how things work.
39. I like meetings or discussions to follow a proper pattern and to keep to a timetable.
40. I don't mind in the least if things get a bit out of hand.

Figure 3.1 Self-analysis questionnaire

To reveal your preferred style/s it is necessary to compute a score for each of the four main styles. Do this by scoring **one** for each statement you ticked (ie, ignore crosses at this stage). The statement numbers are listed in **Figure 3.2**). Add the ticks to get a score for each style:

Activist	Reflector	Theorist	Pragmatist
2	11	1	4
5	12	3	7
8	16	6	9
15	18	10	14
19	21	13	20
23	25	17	24
26	29	22	27
35	30	28	31
36	32	38	34
40	33	39	37
Scores			
—	—	—	—

Figure 3.2 The statement numbers of the four main styles

Now transfer each score onto its appropriate axis on **Figure 3.3**). Link the four points to make a four-sided shape to give you a visual impression of the balance between your preferred learning styles.

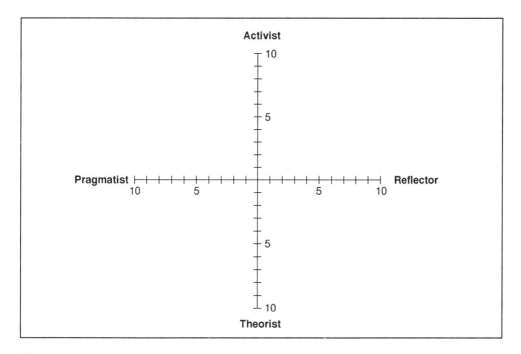

Figure 3.3 Framework for showing the balance of your learning styles

Finally refer to the descriptions of aspects of the styles which follow.

We need to spend a little time considering the results of your learning style analysis. Each learning style has its attendant strengths and weaknesses. Here is a summary of some of them:

Activists, as the name suggests, show an inclination towards action. They initiate and 'get stuck in' enthusiastically but lack staying power and may get bored quickly. They quite like being confronted with new challenges and respond well to leadership roles. They have lots of ideas but are less likely to be good at systematic planning or structured evaluation, and may not be good at listening or maintaining 'hands-off' in a given situation. If you incline strongly in this direction as a teacher you may have a spontaneous, inspirational approach but you may find that methodical lesson preparation, evaluation and record keeping does not come easily to you (not to mention keeping a reflective journal!). How do you think that a student who personally inclines towards the reflective style will react to your teaching?

Reflectors, on the other hand, are likely to be very good at making evaluations and giving feedback but can be flummoxed by being 'put on the spot'. They may appear to lack flexibility and even confidence because they like to weigh situations up and tend not to like to commit themselves until they have had a chance to think through all the angles. They do not respond well to pressure, preferring to go away and think something through with opportunities to research aspects. If you incline towards this style you will probably be happy to spend a lot of time planning and evaluating, but you may find it difficult to respond creatively to unforeseen learning opportunities which might require improvisation. You are probably a good observer and listener and keep careful records. How do you feel that a student who thrives on spontaneity and practical activity would respond to your teaching style?

Theorists tend to be logical and systematic in their approach. They are attracted towards systems, models and concepts and may be bothered by the existence of 'loose ends' and blurred distinctions. They may appear not to be very person-centred in their approach and are uncomfortable if what they are doing does not have a clearly defined purpose. They relish an intellectual challenge and are likely to be suspicious of others' intuitive judgements and responses in a given situation. If you incline strongly towards this style you may have to make a special effort to see the point of view of others who do not see things your way and you may find the slower pace of the less able student frustrating, but you will try to help students tackle problems logically and systematically. You are probably good at providing reasoned justifications and explanations. How do you think a student who lacks confidence would respond to your teaching style?

Pragmatists like to see the point of things and are good at 'getting on with the job'. They have good problem-solving skills and, though they are open to new ways of doing things, they have a strong preference for things they know are going to work. They tend not to like risks and are more likely to play safe in a given situation. They do not respond well to apparently irrelevant ideas, preferring clear connections and relevance. If you incline this way you are unlikely to have an experimental approach in your teaching, preferring to stick to 'tried and tested' approaches. On the other hand, if you are confident of the value of something you will make an effort to incorporate it into your work. You are probably good at cross-examining those who have 'bright ideas'. How do you think a student who seems all the time to want to go about things their own way would respond to your teaching style?

These are dangerously brief summaries. They are 'brief' because we cannot possibly cover all the angles, and 'dangerous' because we would not want to inadvertently give the impression that there are four types of learner and four corresponding types of teacher. These styles express **tendencies** which individuals may display to a greater or lesser degree, and our point here is that if you know about them you are in a position to work with that knowledge to improve the learning of your students. This will involve your being more aware of their needs as learners and simultaneously of your own often subconscious preferences for how to go about things as a teacher. We have already mentioned that as an educated adult you are able to engage in 'thinking about thinking' (metacognition), and your conscious use of this knowledge about learning styles, including a deliberate emphasis of specific styles to suit specific circumstances, would be a case in point.

Action points

In the light of what you now know about learning styles, return to the scheme of work you planned earlier (Chapter 2).

1.   Reappraise the scheme as a whole with learning styles in mind.
2.   Have you favoured any style/s in particular?

3. Have you under-provided for any style/s?
4. Does this matter? (Clearly answers to this will to some extent depend on the context. We are trying to alert you to the issue of preferred learning style, but we do not mean to inadvertently suggest that each style should be given equal emphasis in each and every case.)
5. Make any adjustments to your scheme of work you think are necessary.

Differentiation

In *Beginning Teaching Workbook 2* you were introduced to some classroom observation activities. You will also have undertaken some planning and teaching of learning activities and individual lessons. Your experience in these will have reminded you of some of the differences which exist between individual learners.

Activity

1. Make a list of as many 'axes of difference' as you think of (eg reading age, gender). You may find it useful to refer back to earlier entries in your reflective journal when thinking about this.
2. Compare your list with that of your peer partner.
3. Discuss what the implications of your combined lists are for you both in terms of planning for learning.

Catering for difference

There is a group of differences which can be summarised as relating to ability. Clearly ability has many manifestations, and those who are able in one way may be less able in another. As a consequence of this it is quite likely that an individual will be judged to be at different 'levels' in different subjects of the National Curriculum at any particular time.

In the context of a class, individual learners may well be at different levels of attainment within individual subjects. This is recognised in the rubric of the National Curriculum which states that by the end of each key stage, attainment can be expected to be spread across a range of levels as follows:

Key Stage 1	Levels 1 to 3
Key Stage 2	Levels 2 to 5
Key Stage 3	Levels 3 to 7

From this it follows that in your planning you will need to make provision for learning at different levels, and for your students to be able to demonstrate attainment at a level appropriate to them. This is equally true in the setted/streamed situation (where a degree of homogeneity is assumed), and in the mixed ability/all ability situation (where heterogeneity is acknowledged), though in the latter case the spread or range of ability will probably be greater. In the end, both arrangements result in groups composed of **individuals**, which is what we are concerned with here. This 'matching of work to an individual's abilities' is called **differentiation**.

Differentiation is an aspect of teaching which calls for thought, planning, empathy, knowledge, skill, flexibility and awareness. The cognitive, behavioural and affective aspects of teaching we referred to in *Beginning Teaching Workbook 2* are all in play. We say this not to put you off, but simply to draw attention to the fact that good differentiation is not achieved overnight. It is, however, a crucial aspect of good teaching. Tim Brighouse (1991, p.30) talks of teaching involving a quest to 'find the key to unlock particular children's minds'. To extend his metaphor, the better a differentiator you are, the larger your bunch of keys, as no two children (and no two minds) are the same. And to know which key to use, you have to know your students as individuals.

The theory of multiple intelligences (Gardner, 1983) *proposes that far from there being one sort of intelligence, there are in fact several areas in which an individual can 'be intelligent' and therefore show ability. These are:*
- *linguistic;*
- *logical/mathematical;*
- *musical;*
- *spatial;*
- *bodily kinesthetic;*
- *interpersonal;*
- *intrapersonal.*

Kornhaber et al (1991) suggest that in the West the linguistic and logical mathematical intelligences dominate our thinking about intelligence and therefore our thinking about education to an undue and damaging extent. They argue that in concentrating upon these two forms of intelligence, schooling does not prepare students to meet "the variety of tasks and challenges that human beings confront" and therefore does not fulfil the stated mission of 'preparation for life'.

Two of the most obvious forms of differentiation are:

- *differentiation by task, in which learners are set different tasks according to their ability (eg texts of different 'reading age' about the same body of knowledge);*
- *differentiation by outcome, in which all learners are set the same task and produce a different quality of result according to their level of ability in the task set.*

However, to think that this is all there is to differentiation would be to fall into a false dichotomy of thinking that one can only do one or other of these two things. It is a truism to say that the best teachers know their students. Good teaching is interactive. It also, as 'expert practice', may border on the intuitive. Imagine the situation in which a teacher is explaining something to a class. Most of the class are showing interest but Ajay appears bored. The teacher asks Ajay why he is not paying attention and he replies that he knows about this already because he looked it up in his encyclopaedia. The teacher asks Ajay to tell the class what he knows.

On one level this seems like a common sense reaction to the situation. One might say of the teacher that she was aware of feedback from the class and made an on-the-spot decision to proceed differently, which is good teaching. It is also differentiation, in that in this simple case Ajay has been treated differently from the rest of the class. This differentiation was spontaneous and unplanned (and not necessarily related to ability as such). However, it was also part of a professionally judged response to the situation and hence represents a generalisable and transferable strategy.

Consider another case: Julie is not getting on with her work. The rest of the class are. She does not understand the task. The teacher explains it in a different way, giving Julie some assistance to get her started with her work. This is **differentiation by support**. So, too, is having a support teacher in the room to work with certain targeted individuals on account of their particular needs. We see then that some differentiation by support can be spontaneous, whereas some is planned.

One more case: Chris and Claire are working on similar tasks. They produce similar results. Chris is praised, but Claire is asked to return to her place and give it more thought. It is the best piece of work Chris has done, but in Claire's case the work is not a true reflection of what she can do. This is **differentiation by response** and obviously needs to be handled tactfully and skilfully.

The concept of 'personal best' performance, commonly associated with athletes, is useful here. Differentiation strategies seek to enable each learner to achieve a personal best as often as possible, as a reflection of progress. Some teachers assert that differentiation is therefore just 'good teaching'. We know what they mean, but equally we feel that only by thinking consciously about differentiation in all its different forms can you be sure to incorporate the full range of strategies into your teaching.

Though, as we have indicated, differentiation is very much an issue for the individual teacher to address, there is one set of instances in which the decision is largely taken out of your hands. All schools are legally required to have an explicit policy and 'code of practice' for dealing with any **special needs** as may be manifest or diagnosed in certain students. These special needs are learning difficulties which require additional support. (Note that this additional support includes action on the part of the regular class/subject teacher/s.) We alert you to this here, but will return to it in greater detail in a later section.

Activity: Planning for differentiation

1. Focus on an individual lesson you are soon to teach, with a class you know quite well. Write or modify the lesson plan in the light of what you now know about differentiation.
2. When you have taught the lesson, make a particular point of evaluating those aspects which relate to differentiation.
3. Return to a scheme of work you have planned and think about it in terms of the class/es to whom you will teach it/are already teaching it.
4. Review what you know about the members of the class. Can you find out any more? Are there any individual needs or differences of which you need to take account?

5. Begin to identify those elements of your scheme of work where you may need to make planned provision for differentiation.
6. Consider the practical implications of your thoughts about differentiation in terms of:
   - *grouping strategies in the class;*
   - *preparation and provision of resources;*
   - *collaboration with colleagues, eg support teachers, mentor, student colleague if jointly timetabled.*
7. Discuss aspects of this with your mentor, tutor and peer partner, all of whom will have a perspective on the issue of differentiation.
8. Make an entry in your reflective journal.

Action point

Discuss what you have learnt about differentiation with the school's special needs coordinator or equivalent. Are there other aspects of the school's policies and practices about which you should know?

Summary

In this chapter we have focused specifically on the idea of **learners as individuals**. This has involved us in examining the idea of learning styles by identifying your own preferred learning style. Using this as a basis we were then able to go further into the idea of individual difference, leading to a clear case for the importance of considering differentiation.

Time out: a progress check

We assume that by now you are well into a main teaching practice and that you have taught a number of lessons. If you have worked your way conscientiously through the preceding sections of this workbook you have made progress in many ways, and it is worth taking stock of what you have achieved. (Note that there is no assumption or implication that at this, the approximate half-way point in the book, you are half-way through a main period of teaching practice.)

First, a few questions relating to personal organisation:

- *Are you building up an organised and orderly file of schemes of work, lesson plans and evaluations, originals of 'home-made' resources, together with resource lists and specific reviews?*
- *Are you up to date with your monitoring using the teaching approaches matrix?*
- *Are you keeping abreast of both preparation and marking?*
- *Are you keeping appropriate records of attainment and attendance?*
- *Are you managing your workload effectively, not only to meet deadlines but also to maintain some sort of social or personal life?*

Now, some questions about your teaching:

- *How many lessons have you taught?*
- *Do you know the names of your pupils/students?*
- *Is your main concern your teaching or their learning?*
- *Do your plans demonstrate progression and continuity?*
- *Are you employing a range of differentiation strategies?*
- *How many times have you been formally observed whilst teaching?*

Next, some questions relating to your overall development:

- *Are you keeping up with entries in your reflective journal?*
- *When was the last time you discussed your progress, as opposed to an individual lesson or suchlike, with your mentor?*

The competencies statements are to be found in The Teaching Competency Profile on pages 46–50.

- *When did you last see your tutor, and what did you discuss?*
- *Are you in regular contact with your peer partner, and what did you talk about in your last few meetings?*
- *When did you last read from a book about education (other than one of these workbooks)?*
- *Are you keeping track of how you are developing in the five main areas of competence and against the specific competence statements?*

In a sense there are not particular right and wrong answers to these questions (though some might carry an implication!). Rather, we hope that the activity of addressing them will trigger ideas and responses which will help you to reflect on your development. The positioning of the list of questions here is fairly arbitrary, as most of the questions could be asked at any stage. For that reason we suggest that you use it as another aid to your regular review and target setting. Do not just treat it as a 'one-off'!

It is particularly appropriate to take stock in the way mentioned here before going on to the next chapter in which we offer some suggestions for taking a closer look at your teaching. It is also appropriate here to consider the breadth of what you are currently doing. If basic elements of your work are 'in place' you should now also ensure that the breadth of what you are doing begins to reflect the full breadth of the teacher's role.

Broadening your role

We have assumed in the above progress check that you have certain basic elements of your work as a teacher firmly in place. Another aspect of the review which we are encouraging you to undertake at this stage is that it should lead you to building on what you have achieved by broadening your range of professional responsibilities. Precisely what this looks like will reflect your individual circumstances and your school. However, you should try to extend into at least some of the elements in the following checklist if you have not already done so. Note that at least some of the following can only be done with due regard to school procedures and guidelines, and should therefore not be attempted without consultation, normally with your mentor.

- *Teaching and administrative responsibilities associated with the form tutor/pastoral role;*
- *Participation in reporting and consultation procedures including involvement in parents' evenings;*
- *Organisation and running of some form of extra-curricular activity, such as clubs, societies or teams;*
- *Attendance at school-based in-service education and training (INSET);*
- *Involvement in formal assessment procedures to monitor progress;*
- *Some form of external liaison to arrange, say, a visit out of school or a visitor into school.*

Activity

1. Identify some areas for development from the above list.
2. Discuss your thoughts with your mentor and others as appropriate. Negotiate and agree some ways forward.
3. Formulate an action plan for broadening your experience into agreed areas.
4. Implement your action plan and broaden your role!

Action point

After implementation, review and reflect on the impact on your professional learning of the new, broader aspects of your role. Record your thoughts in your reflective journal.

4
Taking a closer look at your teaching

Aims

In this chapter we aim to help you take a closer look at a number of aspects of your teaching. We cannot be exhaustive, but we can look at some important aspects and, in so doing, give you some ideas for looking at others which might be of interest to you. These aspects we have chosen are:

- *your questioning skills;*
- *your explaining skills;*
- *your classroom management;*
- *the reactions of students to your teaching.*

The assumption here is that you have made progress in these things because you have been doing them for a while. You may even have settled into a routine where you have found out what works for you and where you now feel secure. **Do not relax**. This is just the time to take a fresh look at things and move yourself on to new heights of achievement. Teaching may not be perfectible, but it **is** improvable – indeed, for some teachers their whole career is one continuous search for improvement. This is not some sort of idealistic martyrdom based on a hang-up about their own unworthiness! Rather, it is something like the attitude of the professional researcher, but in this case it is driven by reflective enquiry into their own practice and how they can do better in helping children learn.

Questioning

'... questioning is such an important and ubiquitous activity in the classroom that one should not shirk the task of studying questioning ...', Brown and Edmondson in Wragg (1984). Without doubt questioning and explaining are core skills for any teacher to possess, for they lie at the interactive heart of the teaching role. As skills, though complex in themselves they are both relatively easy to isolate for investigative purposes. And they are both improvable – almost *ad infinitum*.

Do not underestimate the significance (and frequency) of questions. Day et al (1990) quote from an account by Laycock of a school-based development project which carried out some classroom-based research. The group of teachers looking into learning in their school were surprised by 'the sheer number of questions generated by teachers'. It also surprised the teachers who were observed. One teacher said that though she was happy to be observed, there would not be many questions; during 35 minutes 110 questions were recorded!

'A five year old girl returned from her first day at school and announced that her teacher was no good because she didn't know anything. When asked why she thought that, she replied that the teacher just kept on asking us things...' (Brown and Wragg, 1993, p. 3)

'Observers were left with the impression that rather too often questions were just a method teachers had of controlling or dominating a discussion; rather than provoking thought, they could in fact dull the student's receptiveness to the really valuable question.' (Laycock, quoted by Day et al 1990, p. 219).

What can we learn from this? It is clear that the teachers studied were not always aware of the questioning they were doing. Does this mean that they were not really thinking about the questions themselves either? There is a strong implication that it is possible to **over-use** the technique of questioning and that this could be counter-productive. There is also, by extension, a clear suggestion that questioning as a technique can be done well or not so well; it can be used effectively or it can be mis-used.

Brown and Wragg (1993, p. 5) suggest that it is therefore important not only to consider the general use of questions in teaching but also to ask oneself **why** one is asking a certain question, and indeed, why **this** question of **this** student?

Activity

1. Think of as many reasons as you can for asking questions when you are teaching. This will probably be a more productive activity if you 'brainstorm' a list with your peer partner.

Tape recording a lesson can be achieved easily. Many modern cassette tape recorders have an internal microphone and automatically adjust the recording level according to the sound level of the source. Place the tape recorder where it will be out of the way and not noticed by the class, and start it before the lesson begins. You should find that it will pick up your voice clearly from just about anywhere in the room, but it will also indiscriminately record the noise of feet, coughs and sneezes, shuffling of books and papers, moving of furniture, aircraft passing overhead, etc.

Video recording a lesson will give you visual information as well as auditory information. However, a video camera is more likely to excite interest among the class, though our experience is that if the camera is behind them and its purpose is clearly and calmly explained at the start they soon forget about it. If you set up a camera on a tripod you can set it running in the same way as the cassette recorder mentioned above.
If you arrange for someone to operate the camera, this initially makes it even more obtrusive, but if the operator does not draw unnecessary attention to him/herself then once again he or she and the camera are normally soon forgotten. Using an operator has the advantage of being able to follow your movements, zoom in and out and switch the camera off when recording is not required.

2. Tape record a lesson which includes questioning. Count the number of questions you ask. What sorts of questions did you ask? What was their **purpose** (eg, control, finding the level of understanding, review of learning, etc)?

Types of question

You will probably begin to notice from your analysis of your tape recording that your questions differ in a number of ways. Some extremes might be represented by the following:

- *the 'Joyce Grenfell', eg 'now we all found that an interesting talk didn't we everyone?' This question will probably get exaggerated nods from some primary school children keen to demonstrate their perception of what constitutes the 'right' response and their awareness of non-verbal communication, whereas older students will probably respond with bored indifference (and subversive mutterings of 'no');*
- *the 'rabble rouser', eg 'who likes (here teacher chooses a pop star/sports team/personality of the moment)?' at which point a near riot is sparked as the class immediately splits into 'dos' and 'don'ts' who seize passionately on the opportunity to have a free-for-all in which the hapless teacher is instantly marginalised and subsequently ignored;*
- *the 'maze builder', eg 'would anyone, and I'm thinking here in the light of the ideas of the last few lessons, care to hypothesise why tectonic activity, and we all remember what that is, don't we, correlates quite closely, at least at the level of visual correlation between your maps though admittedly we haven't tested it more rigorously with some sort of statistical procedure, with the apparent margins of the crustal plates, always assuming of course that what we refer to here as crustal plates do, and remember this is still a theory although we have come to accept it as fact, actually exist?' This type of question is likely to be met with a stunned silence (or a chorus of 'you what?') before things go rapidly downhill;*
- *the 'guess what's in my head', eg 'who can think of something which lives in or near water, lays eggs and is found in Australia?' which gets a variety of answers of varying degrees of plausibility including 'frog', 'kingfisher', and 'crocodile', but no one guesses the answer (duck-billed platypus) so the teacher has to tell them after all.*

The rather extreme choice of examples above is not accidental. The first is a **closed question** to which there is really only one 'right' answer. It is also **rhetorical** in that it does not really require an answer; in fact, it is barely a question at all, so it does not get much of a response. The second question is an **open question**, at least to a degree. It is also not **directed** and is potentially inflammatory in terms of social allegiances and competitiveness within the peer group, and needs skilled handling if it is not to get an unwelcome level of response. The third has, believe it or not, a simple question to which the 'correct' answer is 'Yes' (or, more likely, 'No') embedded in it somewhere, though that is not the answer the questioner seeks. The question is not well **focused** and is therefore far from clear. The last goes nowhere, having insufficient contact with the children's experience, whilst giving a superficial appearance of inviting active involvement.

Factors influencing questioning

Good questioning is immensely skilful. The well intentioned (but badly prepared) visiting police officer or firefighter in full working dress who addresses a hall full of secondary school students and opens with 'Who knows what my job is then?' is not likely to get much of a response, except possibly from the wag who says 'astronaut.' Good questioning always involves considering these things:

- *the context of the question;*
- *the purpose of the question;*
- *the recipient/s of the question;*
- *the possible answers and other responses to the question;*
- *the response we make to the response which is given to our question.*

These factors, which interact with one another, will all have an impact on how the question is put (and, indeed, whether or not it should be asked at all).

The context of the question refers both to the physical and social/educational setting in which the questioner is working and to the proposed question's relationship to the matter in hand. This inevitably refers both to what has gone before and what comes after. In our example of the visitor above, a 'cold start' question in a hall full of students is not taking sufficient account of the context.

The purpose of the question is closely linked to the previous point about the context. Why is the question being put? In our example the question is clearly intended as an 'ice-breaker', a way of getting started in a rather artificial setting.

The recipient/s of a question always take a risk if they answer it. If they see a question as difficult they risk in their own eyes the prospect of being 'wrong', assuming (wrongly) that the teacher only wants 'right' answers. They also risk 'going public' in front of their peers and may fear their jeering scorn if the answer is not 'right', or their rejection as a 'clever-clogs' or 'creep' if it is. Our wag above took a different sort of risk in seeking peer approval through a challenging response!

The possible answers to a question are clearly important. In our above example the 'right' answer is so obvious that no one wants to give it. The subversive answer is too tempting. We should always think about the possible answer/s, but it would not be true to say that we should only ask questions to which we **know** the answer. We often do not know how a student sees something, or how they feel about something, but it may be vital to their learning to help them to clarify and articulate it through our questions.

The response we make reminds us that this is interactive teaching which cannot all be worked out in advance. We respond to the response we get to our question. Do we 'prompt' to get an answer which is not forthcoming? Do we congratulate? Do we show surprise? Do we reformulate the answer? Do we return with another, more probing question? It all depends on reading the situation and understanding the needs of the individual/group/class.

Much of the discussion of the above five points can be summarised in one word: empathy. If you can empathise accurately with those of whom you ask questions (provided, of course, the learning objectives towards which you are working are clear), you are more likely to be able to:

- ask purposeful, useful questions which address particular learning objectives;
- direct your questions so as to involve members of the class whilst staying 'in charge';
- pitch questions appropriately in terms of level, register (the language used) and focus;
- create a supportive context in which your respondents feel able to answer your questions, by providing them with affirmative feedback;
- assist individuals in their learning by pausing for reflection, by offering prompts, by probing and by rephrasing what they have said.

The question observation schedule

Figure 4.1 is a framework for the observation of questions. Its basis is a classification of questions according to purpose and cognitive level. Brown and Edmondson in Wragg (1984, p. 105) drew on both earlier work and their own work with teachers in proposing that questions whose purpose was essentially to encourage thinking can be divided into five levels according to the cognitive level at which they are directed, from recall (knowledge), through to evaluation. In addition there are, they propose, three other purposes: to encourage speculation; to elicit an affective response; and for management.

Questioning in the classroom is a powerful technique when well used. It fosters talking and as such it contributes to language development and through this the 'making of meaning'. Questioning and answering is also modelling behaviour in that it demonstrates how an issue can be explored by eliciting and valuing views and opinions.

Understanding OFSTED
OFSTED inspectors are asked to make judgements about teachers' methods and are asked to consider whether 'the teacher's use of questions probes pupils' knowledge and understanding and challenges their thinking.' (The OFSTED Handbook, 1995). The guidance goes on to indicate that when observing whole class teaching inspectors should consider how well the teacher manages the situation so as to involve and stimulate all pupils. When observing group and individual work 'inspectors should look at how the teacher interacts with pupils to challenge their thinking and keep the work focused and moving at pace.'

Activity: the question observation schedule

1. Make four copies of the schedule below.
2. Analyse the tape recording you made in the Activity on pages 25/26 by means of the schedule.
3. Arrange with your mentor to observe two lessons with different teachers, in which questioning can be observed. Negotiate with the teachers involved whether they want feedback.
4. Arrange to be observed in a lesson where you are using questioning, and for the observer to complete a copy of the schedule for you. Discuss the observation after the lesson.
5. Put all the results together and consider your findings. What have you learnt about questioning? It may be appropriate to write a brief report, or to make a summary list of action points. Make an entry in your reflective journal.

Class		Teacher			Room		Date		Period/time	
Topic/subject/theme										

Phase of lesson	Type of question								Total questions
	1	2	3	4	5	0	F	M	
1st quarter									
2nd quarter									
3rd quarter									
4th quarter									
Totals									

Cognitive level

1 Data recall including recall of task, procedures, knowledge, values. Naming. Observing Classifying. Reading aloud. Providing known definitions.

2 Simple deductions usually based on data provided.Comparing. Providing simple descriptions and interpretations. Providing examples of principles given.

3 Providing reasons, causes, motives, or hypotheses which do not appear to have been taught in the lesson.

4 Problem solving. Sequences of reasoning.

5 Evaluating a topic, set of values or one's own work.

Speculative, affective response, management

O Speculative, intuitive guesses, creative and open.

F Encouraging expression of feelings and empathy.

M Management of class, groups, individuals, including directing pupils' attention, control, checking that task is understood and seeking compliance.

Figure 4.1 The question observation schedule. The question types have been taken from Brown and Edmondson in Wragg (1984)

Notes on using the question observation schedule (Figure 4.1)

The schedule is designed for the collection of information about **teacher questions only**. To record the occurrence of questions of particular types/levels, the use of tally marks is recommended.

We recommend that you divide the lesson into phases, and have suggested quarters. This is because you might find it interesting to look at how questioning varies through the lesson (Obviously we don't know how long 'a lesson' is in your school, so you will have to sort out the timing!) There is nothing fixed about this, and you might prefer a different sub-division of the lesson or indeed to take the lesson as a whole.

It is important that you identify any specific action points or targets for future work.

Explaining

Explaining is a crucial aspect of skilful teaching. It is the process whereby one person gives understanding to another (Wragg and Brown, 1993). Sometimes an explanation can be **prepared** in advance. Such explaining often occurs in the initial 'exposition' phase of a lesson in association with informing and questioning. In other circumstances the explanation will be **improvised** in response to a set of circumstances.

In reality it is rare for a prepared explanation to be wholly scripted down to the last word, so there are usually improvised elements, often in response to feedback, for instance the rephrasing of something in response to a puzzled look. Equally, even the most apparently spontaneous explanation must have a basis in prior knowledge and thought so, to that extent at least, is prepared.

Activity

1. Arrange a meeting with your peer partner.
2. Arrange to have a cassette tape recorder available for the meeting.
3. Before you meet, each of you should prepare a short explanation of how to do something with which you are familiar, or how something works, to last about five minutes. No props or visual aids are allowed. Prepare your explanation but do not rehearse it.
4. When you meet, each should give the explanation to the other. Tape record the explanations, during which you will observe the following rules:
    * *sit facing one another;*
    * *the explainer may not use body language (gesture, head movement, posture, facial expression);*
    * *the listener may not respond in any way (body language, including movement, grunts, verbally).*
5. When you have both given your explanations, compare your reactions to both roles (explainer and listener).
6. Now review the tape recordings. Try to identify those verbal aspects of the explanations which helped and any which did not.
7. What have you learnt about explaining from this exercise?

Structuring an explanation

'What I tell you three times is true' (Lewis Carroll *The Hunting of the Snark*). Michael Marland writing in *The Craft of the Classroom* (1975, p.72) refers to the old preachers' rule to 'tell them what you are going to tell them, tell them, and then tell them what you have told them'. This is sound advice, and is far from being a recipe for boring your class to death. What it identifies is that a good explanation includes:

* *an introduction, including **advance organisers**. These are structuring 'pointers' given to the listeners so that they have an idea of what is coming and why;*

- a 'body', *including elaboration in which more detail is given about the points listed in the advance organisers;*
- *a conclusion, in which a summary of the explanation is given, including a recapitulation of the main points.*

In other words, the explanation has a clear **structure**. (You may have identified this in the Activity, above.)

...or, as the mother of one of the authors once exasperatedly exclaimed, when her offspring professed not to know what she was 'on about': 'It's perfectly clear to anyone who understands it!' Quite.

This structuring of an explanation is important because, as with good questioning, it shows that we are thinking about the needs of our listeners. They presumably do not know about or understand whatever it is we are setting out to explain to them, so we are empathising with their position and consciously helping them towards understanding by guiding them through our explanation. This increases the likelihood of their being able to follow the explanation in a meaningful way, instead of just going on a 'magical mystery tour'. You will have recognised that, again as with questioning, the pitch (level, register, focus) of an explanation matters.

Activity

Understanding OFSTED
*In making judgements about a teacher's methods, inspectors are asked to consider whether 'exposition or explanation by the teacher is informative, lively and well structured.' (**The OFSTED Handbook, 1995**).*

1. Arrange another meeting with your peer partner. This time if possible arrange for a video camera and tripod to be available.
2. Each prepare a short explanation reflecting part of the requirement of the National Curriculum programme of study for a subject of your choice. Try to structure your explanation helpfully. Previous constraints (see Activity on page 29) do not apply to preparation or presentation.
3. Set up the camera so that you can be filmed whilst addressing your partner (ie, speak to them and not directly to the camera).
4. Give your explanation to your partner; listen to an explanation from your partner. Record both.
5. Before you review the tape, compare your reactions as explainer and listener. What was this experience like compared with the previous, more constrained situation?
6. Now review the video. What did you do or not do which helped or hindered your explanations?
7. What have you added to your knowledge about explaining?

Types of explanations

Many explanations occur in response to questions. Sometimes those questions are stated, either by teacher or student; sometimes they are implicit. The relationship between explanations and questions is emphasised by Brown and Armstrong in Wragg (1984, p.124.). In their typology of explanations, they identify a relationship with particular types of question as follows:

*The types of explanations identified here are all distinct from the **giving of instructions**. That being said, many of the skills and attributes which apply to good explaining also apply to giving instructions, eg in the setting up of learning tasks, clarity and good organisation are important. Giving instructions can be practised away from the class, eg to a partner or to a tape recorder or video camera.*

An interpretive explanation answers questions of the 'what is … ?' variety, by clarifying, exemplifying or interpreting the meaning of terms, for instance 'A duck-billed platypus is an Australian, egg-laying animal which lives …', or 'What we mean by teaching is in fact a complex set of actions involving … '

A descriptive explanation answers questions of the 'how is … ?' or 'how does … ?' variety by describing a process or structure, for instance 'Pain in the human body is detected by certain nerve-endings known as pain receptors, which rapidly pass a message along the nerve to the brain …', or 'A saxophone produces sound by means of the player blowing into the mouthpiece which causes the reed to vibrate very quickly, making a high-pitched buzzing noise …'.

A reason giving explanation addresses questions of the 'why is … ?' and 'why does … ?' variety by offering reasons or causes for the occurrence of a particular phenomenon, for instance 'Seurat is described as a *pointillist* painter because of his use of the technique of building up a painting from thousands of tiny dots or points of pure colour carefully arranged ….' or 'A meteorite burns up when it enters the Earth's atmosphere because friction with the air through which it is passing raises the temperature so much that some of the constituent materials melt and vaporise while others ignite ....'

Skills of explaining

The skills of explaining begin before the explanation itself, at the planning stage. Brown and Armstrong in Wragg (1984, p.123) identify five specific planning strategies including:

- *the analysis of the topic into 'keys', which are those aspects of the topic which can help to unlock its full understanding;*
- *the identification and clarification of links between the constituent parts of the topic which will assist in structuring and sequencing the explanation;*
- *the recognition of any rules, generalisations or principles involved;*
- *the identification of the type/s of explanation which are required;*
- *reflection on the characteristics of the learners (including age, prior knowledge, cognitive skills and motivation) and adaptation of the plan accordingly.*

We have noted above that though some explanations can be planned in advance, some are improvised on the spot. What then happens is that the skilled explainer, far from omitting the above steps, actually goes through them at high speed, often to come up with an explanation which is a finely judged response to the need which has been made manifest by, say, a particular question from an individual child. This may be to turn the entire explanation into a sequence of questions addressing keys and links in a logical succession which enables this specific child, through his or her own answers to the questions, to construct the explanation sought. The observer may see an immediate and appropriate, apparently intuitive response. This can justly be described as 'expert practice'.

Richard Dawkins, Oxford University lecturer in Zoology and writer of **The Selfish Gene, The Blind Watchmaker** *and other books explaining genetics, gives acknowledgement to his students and the tutorial system for helping him practise his skills in 'the difficult art of explaining'.*

Those teachers who are expert at explaining can usually be seen to have internalised what Brown and Armstrong call basic 'performance skills' in explaining. These involve:

- *achieving* **clarity and fluency** *through the definition of terms, the use of clear and explicit language and the avoidance of vagueness;*
- *the establishment of* **emphasis and interest** *by variations in gestures, the use of a variety of media and materials (overhead projector and/or chalkboard to provide visual reinforcement of structure and main points), the skilful use of voice including tone, pace and pauses and by repetition, paraphrasing and the provision of verbal clues;*
- *the* **use of examples** *which are clear, appropriate to the context, 'concrete', and sufficiently numerous to provide support in the development of understanding;*
- *good* **organisation** *including a clear and logical sequence which is organised in a way which is appropriate to the context and uses linking words and phrases;*
- *the provision for, and awareness of,* **feedback** *including giving opportunities for questions, making on-going assessments of whether or not understanding has been developed, and actively seeking the expression of attitudes and values.*

Activity

1. Review what you now know about good explaining.
2. Arrange with your mentor to observe a lesson in which you can focus on explaining. Make notes about the types of explanation, explaining skills and other aspects of explaining which you observe.
3. Arrange to be observed by your mentor or a colleague in a lesson where you will be explaining. Ask your observer to focus particularly on your use of explanation. Discuss the observation after the lesson.
4. Put the results of the last three Activities together and consider your findings. What have you learnt about explaining? Do you agree with Richard Dawkins (see margin, above) that it is a 'difficult art'?
5. It may be appropriate to write a brief report, or to make a summary list of key points in connection with what you now know about explaining. Make an entry in your reflective journal.
7. Identify any specific action points or targets for future work.

Classroom management

As with Richard Dawkins' view of explaining, classroom management also qualifies for the description of 'difficult art'! This can be explained in a single word: **simultaneity**. By this we mean that in a classroom there are many different things happening at once. The 'expert practitioner' may make it appear effortless. Most novice teachers quickly realise just how much is involved.

To the uninformed outsider the teacher may just be 'standing there telling the class while they listen and then they get on with their work'. In reality the teacher is putting into practice a planned sequence of events, yet modifying it in the light of circumstances as they develop, interacting with the class, groups and individuals in it, assessing progress, making judgements about when and how to explain or question, praise or admonish, 'keeping tabs' on individuals' work rates, managing resources and so on!

It is hardly surprising that even those teachers for whom things generally go smoothly find their work tiring. (We mentioned above those expert practitioners who make it appear effortless.) There will be a few, however, who are genuinely gifted, for most it is once again the art which deceives the eye. They have worked hard to get to that position and continue to work hard not just to stay there but to become even better. And, of course, it does not take much for that which is already demanding to become that which is truly stressful.

If your classroom management is going well, it is probably because you are effective in the way you are attending to certain key aspects of your work. On the other hand, if your students are not responding well to your teaching, this may well be manifest in an increasing number of class management issues for you to address. In a study in 1979, Partington and Hinchcliffe identified the following as characteristics associated with effective classroom management:

● *The establishment of good personal relationships characterised by knowing students' names and getting to know them as individual people, responding to them as individuals on the basis of personal knowledge, and by the constructive use of humour;*
● *Effective preparation including being on top of the lesson content and material, being well organised, anticipating problems and having a readiness and appropriate strategies to deal with them;*
● *The organisation of materials and students' work during lessons including the balance between whole class and individual work, an awareness of student movement and an effective use of the teaching space;*
● *Specific pedagogic skills including the skilful use of questions and explanations (see previous two points), the reading of 'cues' from students and making the appropriate responses;*
● *Personal characteristics are to do with how the teacher presents himself/herself. Such aspects may not be easily modified, if at all, but may be crucial in that in extreme cases positive performance on the other four aspects can be negated by certain traits of personality or personal presentation.*

Kyriakou (1991) presents a slightly different arrangement in a list of seven grouped sets of 'essential teaching skills', as follows:

● *planning and preparation;*
● *lesson presentation;*
● *lesson management;*
● *classroom climate;*
● *discipline;*
● *assessing pupils' progress;*
● *reflection and evaluation.*

These seven areas interact with one another, for instance a well prepared lesson which takes account of the evaluation of previous lessons may contribute to a positive classroom climate, and thereby minimise the need to take action to maintain discipline. In this sense, all seven areas will contribute, directly or indirectly, to more broadly defined classroom management. We have addressed aspects of these seven areas at various points throughout *Beginning Teaching Workbooks 2* and *3*. Each 'area' constitutes a chapter of Kyriacou's book (1991), to which we refer you for further detail.

From the foregoing explanation we see that what we are calling 'classroom management' does not take place in isolation. Just try managing a class who have nothing to do! The first thing you would probably do is try to get them occupied! In other words, classroom management is not an end in itself. Its relationship with other aspects of teaching is complex and mutually interdependent. Well planned, interesting, well presented lessons which are pitched at an appropriate level can be the basis for relatively problem-free classroom management. Equally, your classroom management itself provides a vital part of the setting in which your lesson objectives can be met and the intended learning outcomes achieved.

In his study of American teachers Kounin (1970) identified certain teacher attributes and behaviours which seemed to bear a positive relationship to the involvement of students in their work or to the relative absence of classroom management problems.

Withitness involves the teacher being aware of what is going on in all parts of the room, including students beyond those with whom one is working directly. It is described by metaphorical phrases such as 'having eyes in the back of one's head' or having 'teacher's radar'.

Overlapping is Kounin's term for being able to cope with what we referred to as 'simultaneity', ie being able to do more than one thing at a time.

Smoothness applies a textural metaphor to the progress of the lesson. Kounin observed that children stayed on task better if the teacher avoided what he called 'thrusts', which were teacher initiated distractions or interruptions when the children were busy, 'dangles', which were sudden breaks to change from one activity to another, leaving the first unfinished, and 'flip-flops' which involved finishing an activity and then returning to it unexpectedly.

Overdwelling was also to be avoided in that it involved staying on a task or topic for longer than was necessary and thereby losing the pace of the lesson. This is closely connected with **momentum** which refers to the teacher acting positively to maintain the pace of the lesson.

To take this factor of teacher attributes and behaviours further we draw on the work of Hargreaves et al (1975). In it they provide 'pen portraits' of two types of teachers (p. 260ff) whom they term **deviance provocative** and **deviance insulative**. ('Deviance' here means not conforming to work and behavioural norms – more or less what now tends to be called 'disruptiveness'.) The deviance provocative teacher seems to have problems with misbehaviour and in addressing them only seems to make matters worse, whereas the deviance insulative teacher seems to have relatively few problems with the same students.

The deviance insulative teacher identifies disruptive **behaviours** rather than disruptive **students** and concentrates attention on the former. Students involved in misdemeanours are consistently 'dealt with' but in such a way as to enable them to save face. Such a teacher believes that the misdemeanours are not the typical conduct of the student, and communicates this effectively to the student, both explicitly and implicitly.

The deviance provocative teacher, on the other hand, sees disruptive **students** for whom misbehaviour is their normal state, but responds inconsistently by sometimes making an issue out of their behaviour and sometimes avoiding the issue altogether. The expectation of misbehaviour is mutually reinforced on both sides, which leads to worsening difficulties. Fontana (1985) refers to this as the 'demon-effect', which leads to a self-fulfilling prophesy of disruptiveness.

Aspects of the concept of the 'deviance insulative teacher' can be seen as providing the basis for an approach which has come to be known as **positive teaching**. In this the teacher works to a simple and explicit set of principles:

- *good conduct and work are constantly affirmed and rewarded. This applies not only to what might be termed 'good' relative to the norm, but also to the achievement of what we could call 'zero misdemeanours';*
- *there is a simple code of explicit and accepted standards of conduct and behaviour which is rigorously and consistently applied;*
- *non-conformance with the code is dealt with by a consistently applied, progressive set of sanctions.*

Some schools are seen to have success in applying the positive teaching model. If you want to read more about it we refer you to two books by Wheldall and Merrett (1984 and 1989). Please note that throughout all this there is no suggestion from us, explicit or implied, that you should find no problem with classroom management. There will always be management issues to deal with, many of them relating to student behaviour. As long as aspects of your practice as a teacher are not demonstrably deficient, it is not by the existence of 'problems' that you will be judged, but **how you respond to them**.

Activity

1. Review what you have read in this section. It may be useful to do this by arranging to discuss the topic of classroom management with your peer partner. How do the various ways of looking at classroom management summarised here relate to one another? Do some aspects seem particularly useful, and others less so? You may like to make your own list of what you see as 'useful points for new teachers'.
2. Review your own teaching against what you now know about classroom management. Which aspects are strengths in your case? Can you identify why this is so? Are there any areas for improvement? Can you see any ways forward? Produce an action plan.
3. Arrange to discuss classroom management with your mentor. It might be useful if this took place before a lesson in which classroom management was your mentor's focus for observation.

Health warning: Classroom management is complex. It is not amenable to 'quick-fix' solutions, so do not expect miracles. Just because you change your behaviour, do not expect everyone else to immediately change theirs!

The student perspective

Recent public debate has focused on parents as consumers of what takes place in schools. Yet, as a classroom teacher, your primary concern is probably not the parents as 'clients'. Your focus is more likely to be squarely on their children, your students. Indeed, you may on occasions think of the students as consumers of a sort – of your teaching. However, it is relatively rare for an individual teacher to ask this particular group of consumers what they think of the 'product' they are receiving!

This is tricky territory. A direct approach can be seen by students as 'trendy' or an attempt to 'get on their side'. It can be seen by colleagues as potentially undermining by giving students ideas 'above their station', or irrelevant, as the views of 'immature minds'. On the other hand we know of schools which, by establishing a positive climate around the whole issue of evaluation, are able to work in this way with their students. We would not recommend that you seek direct evaluation data of this sort without first discussing it with your mentor. In some circumstances, far from being a breath of fresh air, you could be courting disaster.

There are also research studies which examine what students value in the teaching they are receiving, and there is quite a notable degree of consistency in the results. We will quote from one such study here. The study took place in Australia and involved processing comments from 154 students who were asked to reflect on what they liked best about the teaching they were experiencing. This took place directly after lessons, enabling students to think about the positive characteristics of the way individual teachers went about their work. Analysis revealed that the following list summarises the matters most frequently commented on by students as aspects of teaching of which they approved:

- *explains so you understand, shows us how to do things;*
- *helps with our work;*
- *caring, relates to students, understands what we say;*
- *controls the class well, does not yell;*
- *makes the work interesting and enjoyable;*
- *can joke around, combines humour with learning;*
- *does not rush us or force us, we can work in our own way;*
- *we learn a lot;*
- *knows what he or she is talking about;*
- *fair, straightforward.*

(Margaret Batten in Day et al, 1993)

This list is quite revealing. It suggests that, as suspected by the 'deviance insulative teacher' in the 'pen portrait' on page 33, students want to learn and that they value teaching which is purposeful towards this end, and which does not neglect the human dimension. Beware of fragmenting the list. For instance, 'joking around' is unlikely to win you much success or approval unless it is found in association with the other elements of the list. We would suggest therefore that such a list be used holistically as an additional element of review.

Activity

1. How much of yourself can you see in this 'student profile of the ideal teacher'?
2. What are the reasons for any differences between your perception of yourself and this list?
3. Does this list suggest any areas for development?

It is also useful to consider unsolicited and indirect feedback from your students as another way of getting some indication of their feelings towards you and your teaching. Consider the following questions (you may find it useful to refer to your reflective journal and your lesson evaluations for some additional prompts):

1. In general are your classes fairly cooperative?
2. Do students show enthusiasm and motivation towards their work?
3. Do your students talk to you on their own initiative?
4. Do your students make positive comments about their work or aspects of your teaching?
5. Do your students seem happy in your lessons?

If the answer to these questions is 'yes', then you appear to have a good relationship with your students. However, it may vary from class to class. This might give you something to investigate further. Note that we are not suggesting that a 'no' means you are doing anything wrong: rather, that there is something to look into, perhaps initially through discussion with your mentor.

5

Taking a closer look at the whole curriculum

Aims

'The purpose of a school's curriculum is to support children in their learning'. The aim of this chapter is to 'open up' this statement and to examine some of its implications more closely. This will involve us in thinking about the 'what', the 'why' and the 'how' of the curriculum. In particular, you will explore what this thing called 'the curriculum' is. Is there a generally accepted view of the curriculum? This will lead us to a consideration of what the curriculum is for. That in turn will lead us to consider how the aims and purposes of the curriculum are achieved, and the extent to which it is possible to evaluate this.

What is 'the curriculum'?

It is probably fair to say that there is sometimes a lack of clarity as to precisely what is being discussed when 'the curriculum' is considered. The word itself originates in Latin as being a course for chariot racing in Roman times, and today has a dictionary definition as a course in general and a course of study in particular. In usage amongst teachers and educationalists this would often be too narrow a definition. For most, 'courses' would not normally be referred to as 'curricula' or 'curriculums', but would be referred to simply as 'courses' (or topics or modules). The content of a course would be outlined by the syllabus or, more recently, programme of study, and set out in schemes of work.

For most teachers 'the curriculum' refers to something greater than an individual course to be run or followed. By default this has led in some cases to a perception of the curriculum of any school as being the sum of the courses/topics/modules provided. However, this definition is itself too narrow to be useful in some cases. This has led to some qualification of the term 'curriculum'. For instance, sometimes you may hear reference to **the taught curriculum**, which is the sum of courses etc referred to above. In *Beginning Teaching Workbook 2* we referred to **the hidden curriculum** which we defined as 'the wordless messages the school gives about itself, its values and ethos, deliberately or, more usually, inadvertently'.

Since the 1988 Education Reform Act, we have **the National Curriculum**. We will say more about this shortly, but for the moment we will establish that this is a legal definition of elements (foundation subjects, programmes of study, attainment targets and assessment arrangements) which must comprise part of the taught curriculum of all schools. In addition to the National Curriculum, all schools are legally required to provide religious education (RE), though it does not have the same specified elements as the foundation subjects. The foundation subjects of the National Curriculum, together with RE, comprise **the basic curriculum**.

Schools as organisations

A school's ethos is its distinctive character as expressed through the prevailing spirit and attitudes of the school community.

It is, however, recognised that all schools differ, and that there are many important and desirable aspects of a school's work which do not fall within the basic curriculum as legally set down. In order to provide a more inclusive term than any of the above four definitions, reference is sometimes made to **the whole curriculum**. This comprises all of the aspects mentioned so far, and could be defined thus:

> *For pupils in school at any stage the curriculum is the sum of all that they experience. This encompasses all of the activities which take place in schools, including the formal programme of educational provision, the informal programme of extra-curricular activities, and those aspects of organisation, management and interpersonal relationships which contribute to the development of the school ethos. Pupils learn from all of these (Nottinghamshire County Council Education Committee Entitlement Curriculum Statement).*

The source of the above quotation indicates to us that there is another way of looking at the curriculum: **the entitlement curriculum**. This has a rather different 'feel' from the other definitions, as it is impossible to conceive of an 'entitlement curriculum' without also thinking of someone to whom it is an entitlement: that is, it brings the child into the picture. And 'entitlement' implies that children have a moral right to the curriculum so defined, 'irrespective of the type of school they attend(ed) or their level of ability or their social circumstances' (HMI in Moon and Shelton Mayes, 1994). This in turn implies a moral obligation to ensure that such a curriculum is indeed provided.

Some of the characteristics and components of the whole curriculum are summarised in the accompanying diagram, **Figure 5.1**. It indicates that, in addition to the aspects of the curriculum already mentioned, there are others to be borne in mind when considering the whole curriculum, including what we may refer to as 'cross-curricular elements' (see page 40).

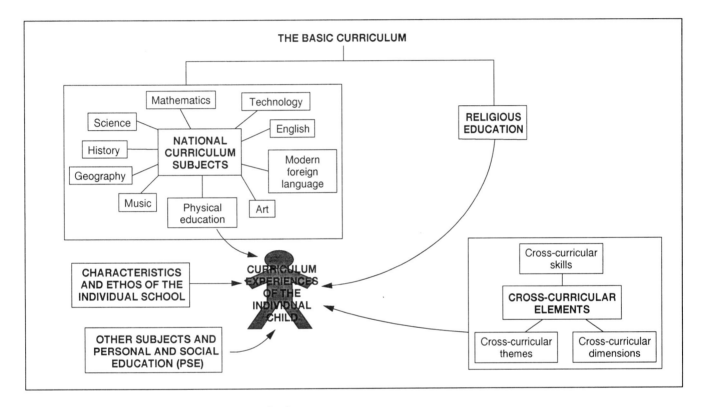

Figure 5.1 Some aspects of the whole curriculum

Figure 5.1 also indicates that at the heart of every curriculum lies the child. This not only reminds us that the sole purpose of the curriculum is to support children's learning, but also that each child is an individual. This means that each child brings to the curriculum a unique set of previous experiences, feelings and capabilities. As a consequence, each child will take meaning from 'curriculum experiences' in a unique way. It is both a sobering and an exciting thought that, no matter how much we may prescribe and try to pin down the curriculum, ultimately there are as many curricula as there are individual children in our schools.

Activity

1. Find out if the school in which you are working has a particular definition of the curriculum. This might be found in the Governors' curriculum statement or policy. Compare it with what you have read in this section.
2. Look at the school's statement of aims or 'mission statement'. Analyse the wording carefully. What is the place of the curriculum in the aims or mission statement?
3. Talk to some teachers. How do they see the meaning of the word curriculum? Is there any indication that their planning and/or other aspects of their work are influenced by how they see the curriculum?
4. What would be your own view on what constitutes a useful definition of the curriculum? It would be a good idea to discuss this with your peer partner, both in order to clarify your thinking and to see whether there is agreement between your definitions.

What is the curriculum for?

The 1988 Education Reform Act (ERA) specifies the nature and purpose of the curriculum as follows:

> Schools must provide a balanced and broadly based curriculum which: promotes the spiritual, moral, cultural and physical development of pupils at school and of society; prepares pupils for the opportunities, responsibilities and experiences of adult life.

In their earlier work on 'the entitlement curriculum' (see, for instance, *Curriculum 11–16*; *Towards a Statement of Entitlement: Curricular Reappraisal in Action* (1983), also known as HMI 'Red Book Three'), HMI and a number of local education authorities had taken a detailed look at the curriculum, its nature and purposes.

In their chapter on 'the entitlement curriculum' in Moon and Shelton Mayes (1994), HMI note that from their work,

> the following argument began to take shape: pupils have common needs to develop, with maximum enjoyment, skills and attitudes necessary for their individual autonomy now and in the future and for work and political and social participation in the democratic society to which they belong; they face the common experience of living in a world which is increasingly international, multi-ethnic and interdependent both economically and politically; their curricula should be based on a common framework which provides coherence, and, while taking account of individual needs and abilities, still ensures the provision of a broadly based common experience.

It follows that if the above describe the curriculum to which all are entitled, then each school has a responsibility for ensuring the provision of a curriculum so described. Thus each school should have a **statement of curricular aims**, which is taken to be 'a general statement of intent', eg 'to develop the skills, knowledge, understandings and attitudes to enable young people to participate effectively in the increasingly globalised world of the future'. Such an aim clearly needs careful 'unpacking' and translating into detailed objectives if it is to be anything other than a worthy sentiment, but taken together such aims provide a statement of purpose of the individual school and should answer the question 'what is the curriculum for?'

Activity

1. Consider the two quotations in this section from the ERA and HMI. In what ways are they different from and similar to one another? Is there any significance in the differences you identify?
2. Refer once again to your school's statement of aims. Does it answer the question 'what is the curriculum for?'
3. Reflect on your experiences so far. Does your school seem to be 'living up to' its aims? Is the school ethos, as you perceive it, congruent with the school's aims?

As before, discussion of the above (for example with your peer partner) will be of value.

How are the aims achieved?

As indicated in the last activity, well thought-out curriculum aims are all well and good, but what really matters is what actually **happens**. In principle, once curricular aims have been agreed the next stage is to set **learning objectives**. On the basis of these, schemes of work (Chapter 2) are constructed, which in turn provide the context for the planning of lessons themselves with specific objectives and intended **learning outcomes**.

Thus it is a question of translating the aims into something which can be put into practice in the classroom and elsewhere. In turn, what is happening in the classroom should support the achievement of the aims. This is why the planning of, say, a new unit of work, should return to the basic questions of 'what are our aims for this work, and how do they fit in with and support our more general stated aims as a school (and, if appropriate, as a department)?'

As indicated in *Beginning Teaching Workbook 2*, it can be helpful to identify learning objectives in terms of skills, attitudes, concepts and knowledge to be learnt, explored, developed, or taught. In such a way the curriculum would overlap the cognitive, behavioural and affective domains shown in **Figure 5.2**. HMI (1983) calls these the **elements of learning**. Seen this way, learning objectives are the crucial link between the planned activities which are the main, overt and practical expression of the curriculum and the aims which guide it.

Clearly the achievement of stated curricular aims for an entire school, be it a small one-class primary school or a huge comprehensive of 2 000 students, requires detailed and careful planning, particularly at the whole-school level. This is particularly the case if we bear in mind the requirements of section 1 of the ERA.

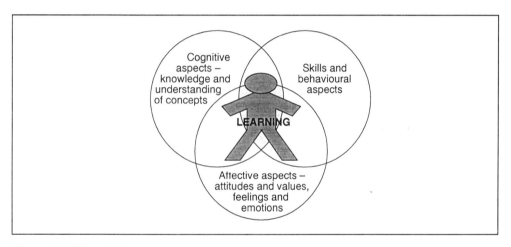

Figure 5.2 The relationship between the three curriculum domains and HMI's elements of learning

Activity

1. Look back at your scheme of work and associated lessons. You may have produced these plans without referring to the school's aims. Analyse your plans, paying particular attention to their aims, objectives and methodology.
2. To what extent are your plans working towards the school's stated aims? Could your plans be improved so as to increase their relationship to the schools aims?

The National Curriculum

In order to move towards the meeting of the general requirements of the 1988 ERA, the National Curriculum was brought into being. It is beyond our scope here to go into detail about what took place but we draw your attention to the fact that elements of the processes and their outcomes were highly controversial and fiercely contested (see, for instance, Bob Moon in Moon and Shelton Mayes, 1994, and Richard Johnson in Education Group II, 1991).

One of the outcomes of the processes of developing the National Curriculum was the reassertion of the primacy of subjects as curricular building blocks, though it was pointed out that there is no obligation on schools to stick to the subject-based model if they want to adopt a different approach to curricular organisation and planning (DES, 1989, para. 3.7). However, the subject-centredness of the eventual documentation, including subject-specific programmes of study and attainment targets makes it more difficult to plan the curriculum in other ways. Some critics of the National Curriculum say that this dominant subject-centredness is backward-looking, particularly in the light of some of the developments associated with the entitlement curriculum. And the DES (1989, para. 3.8) says of the ten foundation subjects that they 'are certainly *not* a complete curriculum; they are necessary but not sufficient ... more will (however) be needed to secure the kind of curriculum required by section 1 of the ERA.'

This leaves schools under an apparent legal requirement to provide more than the minimum stipulated by 'the basic curriculum' (ten foundation subjects plus RE), but with no stipulation in law as to what the 'more' might be. This led to the identification of the **cross curricular skills, themes and dimensions** (see also Figure 5.3) by the then National Curriculum Council (NCC) in England – now subsumed into the Schools Curriculum and Assessment Authority (SCAA) – and the Curriculum Council for Wales (CCW) – now subsumed into the Curriculum and Assessment Authority for Wales (ACAC).

These 'elements' are an embodiment of some basic principles of the curriculum and most will be found in some shape or form in all areas.

It will be useful if you can find the statement of cross-curricular elements which applies in your area, if appropriate. You could then use these as a basis for comparison with the above classification.

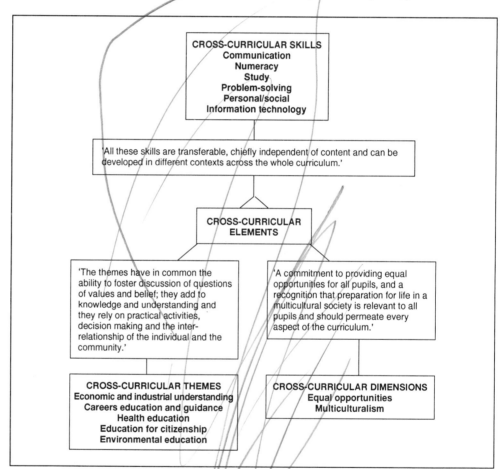

*In **Figure 5.3**, all quotations are from **Curriculum Guidance 3: The Whole Curriculum** (1990), NCC.*

Figure 5.3 The cross-curricular skills, themes and dimensions as originally identified by the National Curriculum Council in England.

Information about these cross-curricular elements was issued to schools in the form of 'Guidance' which, unlike the foundation subjects, was not statutory other than through an interpretation of what was needed in order to meet the general requirements of the ERA. The Guidance had neither attainment targets nor programmes of study. Though as a consequence the Guidance did not have the same status as the Orders for the foundation subjects, some saw the open nature of the Guidance as an opportunity for schools to take the initiative in terms of curriculum development (see, for example, Dufour, 1990, and Buck and Inman, 1992).

However, at the same time as the Guidance was being 'drip fed' into schools, so more foundation subjects were coming 'on stream', and it soon became clear that in many schools the priority was to meet the more clearly stated legal requirements of the foundation subjects. It was also becoming clear that the subject Orders were too detailed and too demanding of time. The taught curriculum was in serious danger of becoming so overcrowded by the statutory requirements of the National Curriculum as to be unworkable, let alone leave time available for any other aspects, whether legally required or merely desirable. This resulted in the *Dearing Review of the National Curriculum* of 1993, and a subsequent 'slimmed down' National Curriculum which came into force for Key Stages 1 to 3 in 1995.

Meanwhile official attention had rather slipped away from the cross-curricular skills, themes and dimensions, which were in any case beyond the strict definition of the National Curriculum as such. Individual schools and teachers had, however, retained a commitment to the maintenance and development of at least some of them, though this was difficult to resource and coordinate for reasons touched on above. The result is that the development of the cross-curricular elements, originally identified as being important additions to the National Curriculum in order to make it 'whole' and thereby satisfy the requirements of section one of the ERA, is, in the experience of the writers, patchy.

It is also possible that the NCC's guidance did not go far enough. Dufour (1990) feels that several current social movements and concerns are not represented in NCCs version of themes and dimensions, and therefore suggests the following list of themes and dimensions, including some of NCC's themes and dimensions in a somewhat different guise:

- *pre-vocational and vocational education;*
- *personal and social education;*
- *health education;*
- *media education;*
- *peace education;*
- *gender education;*
- *multi-cultural and anti-racist education;*
- *global education;*
- *environmental education;*
- *trade union education;*
- *human rights education.*

Activity

1. Choose one of the cross-curricular elements from the above bulleted list or from Figure 5.3. Choose one which is of interest to you and which will extend your professional learning and experience. Find out what you can about your chosen cross-curricular element, for example, from the NCC's Curriculum Guidance series (Books 3 to 8 deal with *The Whole Curriculum* and each of NCC's five themes in turn), the relevant chapter of Dufour (1990) and any other published material or local guidance.
2. Choose one of the National Curriculum subjects. Choose the programme of study for a key stage appropriate to your teaching. Analyse the programme of study for opportunities to develop the place of your chosen cross-curricular element. (We are assuming here that you have set yourself a higher level of challenge than, say, identifying the link between the programme of study for mathematics and numeracy as a cross-curricular skill!)
3. Review your scheme of work in the light of your chosen cross-curricular element. Could you develop your plans in relation to your chosen cross-curricular element? Discuss your thoughts with your mentor.
4. For some lessons you have not yet taught, increase the priority given to your chosen cross-curricular element in your plans. After you have taught the lessons make it a specific focus of your lesson evaluation procedures.

Action points

1. Find out if your school has a coordinator for cross-curricular work in general, or for your chosen cross-curricular element. If so, arrange a meeting where you can discuss your experience regarding the relationship between your chosen cross-curricular element, the National Curriculum and your teaching.
2. It will be useful to discuss all of the above with your peer partner, particularly if he or she has been looking at a different cross-curricular aspect or works in a different school or subject area.
3. Do not forget to write up your thoughts about your experiences and your learning in your reflective journal.

Curriculum evaluation

Processes of curriculum evaluation are really the 'review/plan/do' cycle operating at a different scale (see **Figure 5.4**). And of course, all the scales of review, from the lesson evaluation up, have the potential to feed into and inform processes of curriculum review. Unfortunately it is not quite as simple as that! If, for instance, we take from section 1 of the ERA the requirement that the curriculum 'prepares pupils for the opportunities, responsibilities and experiences of adult life', then the evaluation of the extent to which this is achieved is difficult, not least because of the time lag involved and the problem of collecting appropriate data. So, what was true for lesson planning is, in this sense at least, true for the curriculum as a whole: clear objectives with measurable outcomes are easier to evaluate. (Note that this is not to say that all aspects of 'the whole curriculum' should be or indeed could be reduced to objectives with measurable outcomes.)

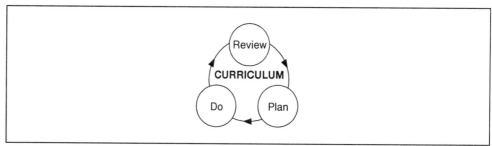

Figure 5.4 The cycle of curriculum review

League tables have focused attention on results as indicators of a school's performance. By implication this means the match between curricular aims and the degree to which they are met, at least in the sense that presumably no school sets out to encourage its students to do anything other than their best. However, league tables indicate just how difficult reliable curriculum evaluation actually is. The data may appear to be 'objective' and standardised but interpretation is very difficult because of the variety of factors influencing this single measure of 'output quality'. There is a debate about just how appropriate league tables actually are, and whether they tell us anything useful (or even anything at all). On the other hand, to the teacher in a classroom, test or examination results can be interpreted in the light of accumulated knowledge about an individual's capabilities and can usefully add to the evaluation of teaching and learning.

*The term **review** is being used here to describe a process which involves both:*
- *the collection of data about something of interest or concern, sometimes referred to as 'auditing';*
- *the subsequent making of judgements on the basis of data collected, ie 'evaluation'.*

The phrase 'curriculum review' carries a clear implication of something more than the sum of individual teachers evaluating their own work. 'Curriculum review' suggests coordination and some sort of over-view. Also, because individual teachers give expression to aspects of the curriculum, the phrase also implies some sort of collaboration or collective activity between these individuals. As Tim Brighouse (1991, p. 30) puts it, 'collective self review would be necessary simply to reflect collectively the individual critical intellectual curiosity of each successful member of staff.' So this sort of review is also an affirmation, a validation of the reflective enquiry undertaken by individual members of staff, in addition to whatever the stated purpose or focus of the review may be.

The point about 'purpose or focus' is important. Elsewhere in the same book (p. 39) Brighouse makes the vital point that 'You cannot review everything simultaneously.' Just as we encourage you in these books to 'action plan' by setting development priorities on the basis of your own review and evaluation, so it is for schools when reviewing their curricula. Development planning cannot focus on everything at once, so priorities have to be set.

Activity

1. Arrange to talk to the Head Teacher (or possibly the relevant Deputy Head or senior teacher with responsibility for curriculum overview in a large school) about the place of curriculum in the school's management/development plan.
2. You may find it helpful to structure your discussion around the following questions:
    ●   *What are the school's current development priorities for the curriculum?*
    ●   *Who is responsible for carrying out the necessary work?*
    ●   *How is the work being carried out?*
    ●   *What support is being given?*
    ●   *How long is the work expected to take?*
    ●   *How will the results of the work be evaluated?*
    ●   *What is the nature of the curriculum evaluation currently in hand?*
3. The answer to the last question may provide you with some follow-up possibilities. Talk to someone so identified about current evaluation:
    ●   *How is it being undertaken?*
    ●   *What criteria are being employed?*
    ●   *What will be done with the results of the evaluation?*

The answers you have received to some of the above questions should enable you to get a 'feel' for this aspect of the culture of your school. You may wish to reflect on the extent to which your school could be described as a **learning organisation**.

Breadth and balance: areas of experience and personal and social education (PSE)

In its work in the 1970s and 1980s, HMI identified six characteristics which it felt should be evident in a school's curriculum (see, for instance, HMI, 1989). They are:

●   *breadth;*
●   *balance;*
●   *relevance;*
●   *coherence;*
●   *differentiation;*
●   *progression and continuity.*

These terms amount to a list of 'general criteria' for making judgements about the curriculum. All require discussion, clarification and further definition if a school is to use them as the basis for detailed evaluation processes. We have looked at some of these characteristics in greater detail earlier in this book and will add a little here in respect of **breadth** and **balance**.

Breadth and balance are quite difficult to define, and any definition reflects subjective value positions about the curriculum. In its work referred to earlier, HMI suggested an interesting way of examining curricular breadth and balance by identifying eight **areas of experience** (see HMI, 1983 and 1989) which should be present in the curriculum. In alphabetical order, so as to imply no hierarchy or precedence, they are:

●   *aesthetic and creative;*
●   *human and social;*
●   *linguistic and literary;*
●   *mathematical;*

The role of criteria in evaluation
Evaluation implies the making of judgements, which in turn implies the existence of some sort of criteria against which such judgements can be made. If evaluation is a systematic process, then at some stage the criteria against which judgements are to be made must themselves be made explicit. If this does not occur, review remains a reflective activity inside people's heads, and true collective review is then difficult to achieve.

These areas of experience, though not the same as the multiple intelligences identified in Gardner's theory of multiple intelligence (see margin note on p. 21), certainly give an echo of this more broadly-based view of intelligence and therefore learning needs/curriculum experiences

- *moral;*
- *physical;*
- *scientific;*
- *spiritual;*

to which list was later added:

- *technological.*

These, it was stressed, are not necessarily congruent with subjects as currently defined, but should help in the selection of knowledge to be covered. This knowledge is in turn the carrier and context for the development of the other elements of learning – skills, concepts and attitudes.

The areas of experience continue to be a useful way of examining breadth and balance in the curriculum, particularly bearing in mind the imperfect relationship identified earlier between the subject-based National Curriculum Orders and the broader requirements of the ERA. Indeed, the Curriculum Council for Wales in its publication *The Whole Curriculum* (which parallels the National Curriculum Council's *Guidance 3: The Whole Curriculum*) reinterpreted the subjects of the National Curriculum in the light of the areas of experience.

Ultimately the purpose of the broad and balanced curriculum is to support the requirements of the ERA to 'promote the spiritual, moral, cultural, mental and physical development of pupils at the school' and to prepare them 'for the opportunities, responsibilities and experiences of adult life'. The ERA formalises what has been in many schools' aims, explicit or implicit, for a long time. Many schools and teachers have articulated this as supporting the **personal and social development** (PSD) of young people. In some schools this is expressed as the over-arching aim of the curriculum, to which subjects, cross-curricular elements, other aspects of the taught curriculum, pastoral work, clubs, societies and teams, the hidden curriculum and all other aspects of life in school contribute (see particularly **Equality Assurance in Schools**, The Runnymede Trust, 1993). In some cases their review procedures have led them to formalise aspects of curricular provision for this aim in programmes of **personal and social education** (PSE) (see Brown in Dufour, 1990, and Best et al, 1995).

Activity

1. Explore your school's definition of PSE and/or PSD. This may involve looking again at the school's aims from this perspective, in addition to talking to someone with a coordinating responsibility or, in the smaller school, to the Head Teacher.
2. How are PSE and PSD organised, monitored and evaluated in your school?
3. Critically reflect on your own broad practice as a teacher. What contribution are you making to PSE and PSD? Develop an action plan to review and develop this aspect of your practice.

6
Review

In *Beginning Teaching Workbook 3*, we have attempted to provide you with some appropriate guidance and support to develop your practice as a 'beginner teacher'. As in *Beginning Teaching Workbook 2*, we have argued that 'it is possible to focus on specific aspects of your development whilst at the same time remaining aware of the larger picture of education as a field of human endeavour with its own dynamic body of professional knowledge'. We have again suggested that 'in your development as a teacher it will be useful if, in addition to developing the competencies which you are required to demonstrate, you bring critical thinking and reflectiveness to bear, both on your own development and on the broader circumstances in which you are working and learning'.

Beginning Teaching Workbook 2: Beginning Initial Teacher Training

We assume that you have already successfully completed a main teaching practice placement and recommend that you now take stock of what has been achieved. The following list of review activities will provide a useful basis.

1. Look back at previous review activities, including those which you conducted at the end of *Beginning Teaching Workbook 2* and the 'progress check' undertaken part-way through this workbook (see pages 23–4).
2. Add to the list of achievements you have made since beginning your entry into teaching (see *Beginning Teaching Workbook 2*). Now as then, this is a serious and worthwhile task, as it is sometimes human nature to tend to focus on problems and on what has yet to be done, rather than affirming achievements. You continue to be involved in a process of professional **and** personal development and change, and may not recognise what you have already achieved unless you focus on it specifically.
3. Re-read what you have written in your reflective journal. Are there any 'patterns' or particular interests, themes or concerns?
4. Refer to the list of competencies on pages 46–9. Are there any with which you feel you still need to make progress? What are your mentor and HE tutor's views about your development of teaching competencies?
5. Review your recent reading. What have you read which has seemed particularly appropriate or useful, or which has provided you with interesting 'food for thought'? Have you discussed your reading with anyone (eg peer partner)?
6. Arrange an end-of-practice review discussion with your mentor. Negotiate an agenda which includes an opportunity for you to speak about:
   * *what you feel you have achieved;*
   * *where you feel you now stand vis-à-vis the competencies;*
   * *any concerns or questions you might have.*
7. Find out whether your mentor wants some feedback from you regarding his or her practice as mentor. (We indicated in *Beginning Teaching Workbook 2* that ideally your relationship is that of a 'learning partnership' in which you both gain insight and develop your respective practice.)

Action planning

In the light of the results of all of the above, formulate an action plan for the next phase of your development (see *Beginning Teaching Workbook 4*). This action plan will take account of:

Beginning Teaching Workbook 4: Pre-entry to First Teaching Post

* *your achievements to date;*
* *your needs as they stand at present;*
* *your profile of competencies as it now stands;*
* *your personal interests regarding aspects of education;*
* *any constraints or external factors (eg remaining assessment deadlines).*

Try to write an action plan which identifies:

* *a new set of appropriate targets;*
* *the date and means by which such targets will have been met;*
* *the evaluation criteria by which you will judge the achievement of your targets.*

You may find that the action planning activity can be undertaken effectively with your peer partner, each of you offering support to the other in the process. Remember too that your action plan should not be 'set in stone'. It is a working framework and as such is open to review and modification as the situation continues to unfold and develop.

The Teaching Competency Profile

Working with the competency profile

The Appendices to **The Management File** *contain the four competency profiles which have been published by the relevant Departments for Education to guide initial teacher training – two in England and Wales (1992) and one each in Scotland and Northern Ireland (1993).*

Before you become an NQT you will be expected to demonstrate your knowledge, skills and understanding of teaching and education against a set of broadly defined competencies. We emphasise that it is not the piecemeal acquisition of individual competencies which will enable you to become an effective teacher. You might find it more useful to think about the 'artistry' of teaching, ie the unique combination of these individual competency statements which together enable you to make professional judgements about pupils and their learning on a daily, termly and yearly basis. But remember that 'the whole' (ie good teaching) is greater than 'the sum of the parts' (ie the competency statements).

The following competency profile is for you and others involved in your ITE to use to evaluate your progress and to set targets for your on-going professional development.It is based on the DFE Circular, *The competencies expected of a newly qualified teacher* (1992). *Beginning Teaching Workbook 5: First Year of Teaching* and *Beginning Teaching Workbook 6: Beyond the First Year of Teaching* both provide developed versions of a competency profile. There may well be a locally available alternative, provided by your school, Higher Education Institution or Local Education Authority. The profile is a framework within which you can monitor your progress. It is not intended as a finite list of teaching competencies which you simply 'work your way through'. Discuss the profile with your mentor: there may be elements which you wish to adapt, remove or add depending on the circumstances in which you are both working. *Beginning Teaching Workbooks 2* and *3* indicate specific points when we recommend you use the profile, but you should see it as a flexible document which is here to support you.

Personal attributes

In using this profile we are making some assumptions about the personal attributes, including attitudes and values, which you bring with you and are seeking to develop through your ITE.

1. Personal attributes

You have:
- a lively mind and a wide range of interests
- the capacity and willingness to continue to learn
- the capacity to justify decisions you make and reflect on your actions

2. Professional attributes

You have the capacity to:
- evaluate your work and set yourself appropriate targets
- engage in a dialogue with others involved in your ITE about your professional development
- participate in a process of critical reflection and on-going development, supported by feedback received from other professionals, eg mentors and tutors
- maintain an interest in the subject matter you are teaching and keep up to date with current developments

3. Professional attitudes and values

You are a person who:
- is committed to learning as a life-long process, and enthusiastic about the contribution which teaching can make
- seeks to foster the development of the whole child
- demonstrably both cares about and likes children
- actively supports equal opportunities policies and practices whilst recognising and catering for individual differences and needs

4. Communication skills and quality of relationships

You can:
- communicate with children and adults easily and effectively
- respond to children in a way that is sensitive to their circumstances
- establish and maintain effective working relationships with students, colleagues, parents and others engaged in the support of students and their learning

Your notes

5. **Personal effectiveness**

You can:

- organise your work effectively
- manage conflicting demands on your time and meet deadlines
- apply knowledge, skills and understandings across a range of circumstances

The competences

Curriculum knowledge, planning and preparation

1. **Plan and prepare lessons using your knowledge and understanding of:**
   - the knowledge concepts and skills of the subjects you are teaching
   - the requirements of the National Curriculum in the subjects you are teaching
   - the overall structure of the scheme(s) you are currently teaching

2. **Plan and prepare lessons which are appropriate to the needs of the individuals and groups and provide progression and continuity of learning by:**
   - setting achievable objectives
   - building on students' previous learning
   - differentiating tasks (on the basis of level of difficulty, pace of work, classroom support and learning styles)

3. **Plan and prepare lessons which take account of the development of the students as a whole person by:**
   - contributing towards the development of students' numeracy, oracy and literacy skills
   - taking into account where relevant the cross curricular themes as identified in the National Curriculum
   - developing social skills alongside academic skills in the process of learning
   - taking account of the contribution different subject areas make to the whole curriculum

4. **Enhance the students' knowledge skills and understanding through:**
   - the use of resources which are appropriate to the objectives being taught
   - the appropriate use of resources in relation to the learning activities within a phase of a lesson

5. **Consult and plan with support staff by:**
   - knowing where to go for help and advice about students who have special needs
   - having a clear understanding of the roles of learning support staff within your school

Classroom management and organisation

1. **Ensure that beginnings and ends of lessons are managed effectively; also that the transitions from one activity to another within them are smooth by:**
   - ensuring the orderly entry, registration and exit from classes
   - waiting for the attention of all students before beginning or continuing to speak
   - organising resources and materials well in advance
   - having well planned lessons with clear objectives for each activity

	Your notes
2. Use a variety of teaching and learning styles by: • matching teaching styles to learning objectives • using whole class, group, paired and individual activities as a means of achieving particular learning objectives • devising learning activities which challenge student thinking • providing opportunities for student–student interactions **3. Provide opportunities for students to take responsibility for their own learning by:** • creating opportunities for self managed learning • providing support for that learning by making advice, materials and equipment readily available • promoting an atmosphere in which students are not inhibited by self doubt and fear of failure • encouraging open discussion and debate **4. Establish and maintain a positive attitude towards students based on mutual respect and freedom from prejudice and discriminatory behaviour by:** • discouraging stereotyping • promoting equal opportunities for all students • valuing students as individuals and enhancing their self-esteem through verbal and non verbal communication **5. Enhance the quality of teaching and learning by:** • the use of a range of resources • the development of own resources which are well presented and accessible to the range of abilities being taught • the appropriate use of IT and other technology in the classroom • providing opportunities for pupils to use resources such as the school library **6. Maintain students' interest, attention and involvement by:** • setting appropriate objectives • using accessible and well presented resources • ensuring that lessons are relevant to the interests, age and ability of the pupils in the class **7. Communicate clearly with the class by:** • using a language register which is appropriate to the age and ability of the students • making appropriate use of verbal and non verbal communication • using questions to develop students' understanding and enhance their own communication skills • using your subject competence as a basis for well structured, unambiguous and clearly delivered explanations **8. Manage classroom behaviour in such a way as to sustain a purposeful working atmosphere by:** • being familiar with the school's policy on student behaviour • consistently applying routines and conventions in the classroom • encouraging and promoting positive behaviour through the use of the school sanctions and rewards system • planning classroom activities which minimise the opportunities for inappropriate behaviour • having clear and realistic expectations which are applied consistently • seeking support when necessary to maintain order in the classroom	

9. **Stimulate and maintain an interest in learning by:**
   - communicating personal enthusiasm for teaching and for the subject matter
   - making learning relevant and purposeful
   - ensuring that learning is well paced
   - taking into account the characteristics of learning groups and their dynamics
   - using pause and silence to good effect

Assessing, recording and reporting on student learning

1. **Monitor and assess students' work using formative methods by:**
   - setting and marking work regularly
   - giving constructive feedback in which the emphasis is on how students can improve their performance
   - monitoring students' progress by evaluating and recording evidence of their learning
   - using the formative assessment process to begin to identify the learning needs of individual students

2. **Involve students in the assessment process by:**
   - helping them to evaluate their own learning
   - using self assessment to complement teacher assessment
   - negotiating short term and medium term learning objectives with students

3. **See assessment as part of the self evaluation process by:**
   - using the outcomes of assessment to inform decisions about the success of teaching and learning
   - using the outcomes of assessment to inform decisions about future teaching

4. **Assess and keep records which are consistent with departmental and school policy by:**
   - being familiar with departmental and school policy on marking, assessment and homework
   - beginning to understand the statutory requirements on marking and record keeping

5. **Find out about the school's policy on reporting by:**
   - reading the school policy and procedures on reporting in the light of national requirements on reporting to parents
   - observing and working within the school's policy on reporting as appropriate

Self-evaluation and professional development

1. **Evaluate lessons to promote students' learning by:**
   - being consistent in the process of evaluation
   - using different sources of feedback as a basis on which to make judgements about the quality of teaching such as:
        - feedback from pupils
        - evidence from work completed by pupils
        - feedback from mentor/tutor/other teachers
        - own response to the lesson

	Your notes
2. **Set appropriate targets for professional development by:** • using informed critical reflection on your work as a teacher as a basis for setting achievable targets • responding positively to constructive feedback • using discussions with mentor/tutor as the basis for establishing appropriate courses of action for achieving targets • taking responsibility for your own professional development ## Whole child/whole curriculum 1. **Demonstrate an understanding of and commitment to the school's pastoral work by:** • appreciating the personal and social needs of students as individuals • taking on aspects of the role of tutor, including working within the school's administrative procedures and guidelines • recognising the contribution of parents to the pastoral work of the school 2. **Begin to appreciate the implications of the 'hidden curriculum' for students by:** • recognising the impact of peer pressure on students • recognising the importance of the quality of student–student and teacher–student relationships 3. **Begin to develop a knowledge and understanding of the school as an organisation and its place within the local community including its:** • organisational structure • day to day management • relationships and communications with parents • links with industry and the wider community 4. **Begin to understand the professional, contractual and legal responsibilities of a teacher by:** • finding out about the role and activities of professional associations • participating, where relevant, in any INSET opportunities provided by the school	

Other notes, comments and targets:

A Lesson Observation Schedule

Name of student teacher ....

Name of observer... Role/position...............................

Class observed .... Room .... Date ....

Topic/theme ....

The student teacher should indicate in this box **before an observation** any particular areas for observation and feedback in the light of review and reflection on progress to date

Also any necessary background for the observer, eg aspects of previous lesson/s

---

Note: The headings of the first three boxes following correspond to areas of the competency profile, to which users are referred for 'prompts'. Observers will wish to have a copy of the appropriate lesson plan and any materials, notes, etc for reference during the lesson

Curriculum knowledge, planning and preparation

Classroom management and organisation

Assessing, recording and reporting on student learning

Other observation notes

Self-evaluation and professional development (see also the competency profile for prompts)

Comments by the student teacher

Other notes, recommendations and agreed targets

Signed: .... (observer) .... (student)

BIBLIOGRAPHY

Bell, L. and Day, C. (eds) (1991) *Managing the Professional Development of Teachers*, Milton Keynes, Open University Press.

Best, Lang, Lodge and Watkins (eds) (1995) *Pastoral Care and Personal Social Education*, London, Cassell.

Bloom, B.S. (ed) (1956) *Taxonomy of Educational Objectives, Cognitive Domain*, New York, David McKay.

Brighouse, T. (1991) *What Makes a Good School?* Stafford, Network Education Press.

Brown, G. and Wragg, E.C. (1993) *Questioning*, London, Routledge.

Buck, M. and Inman, S. (1992) *Whole School Provision for Personal and Social Development: The Role of the Cross Curricular Elements*, The Centre for Cross Curricular Initiatives, Goldsmith's College, University of London.

Careers and Occupational Information Centre (COIC) *Coaching for Managers* (1990), Sheffield, HMSO.

Day, C. Pope, M. and Denicolo, P. (eds) (1990) *Insights into Teachers' Thinking and Practice*, London, Falmer.

Day, C. Calderhead, J. and Denicolo, P. (eds) (1993) *Research on Teacher Thinking: Understanding Professional Development*, London, Falmer.

Dawkins, D. (1988) *The Blind Watchmaker*, London, Penguin.

DES (1988) *Education Reform Act*, London, HMSO.

DES (1989) *National Curriculum: From Policy into Practice*, London, HMSO.

Dufour, B. (ed) (1990) *The New Social Curriculum: A Guide to Cross Curricular Issues*, Cambridge, Cambridge University Press.

Education Group II (1991) *Education Limited*, London, Unwin Hyman.

Fontana, D. (1985) *Classroom Control*, London, The British Psychological Society in association with Methuen.

Gardner, H. (1983) *Frames of Mind: The Theory of Multiple Intelligences*, New York, Basic Books.

Hargreaves, D. Hester, S. and Mellor, J. (1975) *Deviance in Classrooms*, London, Routledge & Kegan Paul.

HMI (1983) *Curriculum 11–16: Towards a Statement of Entitlement: Curricular Reappraisal in Action*, London, HMSO.

HMI (1989) *The Curriculum 5–16: Curriculum Matters 2*, London, HMSO.

Honey, P. and Mumford, A. (1992) The Manual of Learning Styles, UK, P. Honey.

Johnson, R. 'A New Road to Serfdom? A Critical History of the 1988 Act' in *Education Limited*, Education Group II (1991), London, Unwin Hyman.

Kolb, D. (1984) *Experiential Learning: Experience as the Source of Learning and Development*, Englewood Cliffs, NJ, Prentice Hall.

Kornhaber, M. and Gardner, H. in Maclure, S. and Davies, P. (eds) (1991) *Learning to Think, Thinking to Learn*; Oxford, Pergamon Press (for Organisation for Economic Co-operation and Development – OECD).

Kounin, J. S. (1970) *Discipline and Group Management in Classrooms*, New York, Holt, Rinehart & Winston.

Kyriacou, C. (1991) *Essential Teaching Skills*, p. 8–9, Cheltenham, Stanley Thornes.

Marland, M. (1975) *The Craft of the Classroom*, London, Routledge.

Moon, B. and Shelton Mayes, A. (1994) *Teaching and Learning in the Secondary School*, p. 232, London, Routledge (in association with the Open University).

National Curriculum Council (1989, etc) *Curriculum Guidance Nos 3 to 8*, York, NCC.

Office for Standards in Education (OFSTED) (1995) *The OFSTED Handbook* p. 73, London, HMSO.

Runnymede Trust (1993), *Equality Assurance in Schools*; Staffordshire, Trentham Books for the Runnymede Trust

Wheldall, K. and Merrett, F. (1984) *Positive Teaching: The Behavioural Approach*, London, Allen and Unwin.

Wheldall, K. and Merrett, F. with Houghton, S. (1989) *Positive Teaching in the Secondary School*, London, Paul Chapman.

Wragg, E.C. (ed) (1984) *Classroom Teaching Skills* p. 19, London, Croom Helm.

Wragg, E.C. and Brown G. (1993) *Explaining* p. 3, London, Routledge.